SURVIVE
THE FIVE

UNOFFICIAL
PRO GAMER TIPS FOR FANS OF
FIVE NIGHTS AT FREDDY'S

ANNA MIRABELLA

Sky Pony Press
New York, New York

Sky Pony Press books may be purchased in bulk at special discounts
for sales promotion, corporate gifts, fund-raising, or educational
purposes. Special editions can also be created to specifications.
For details, contact the Special Sales Department, Sky Pony Press,
307 West 36th Street, 11th Floor, New York, NY 10018 or
info@skyhorsepublishing.com.

Sky Pony® is a registered trademark of Skyhorse Publishing, Inc.®,
a Delaware corporation.

Visit our website at www.skyponypress.com.

10 9 8 7 6 5 4 3 2

Library of Congress Cataloging-in-Publication Data is available on file.

Hardcover ISBN: 978-1-5107-7552-7
Ebook ISBN: 978-1-5107-7599-2

Printed in China

TABLE OF CONTENTS

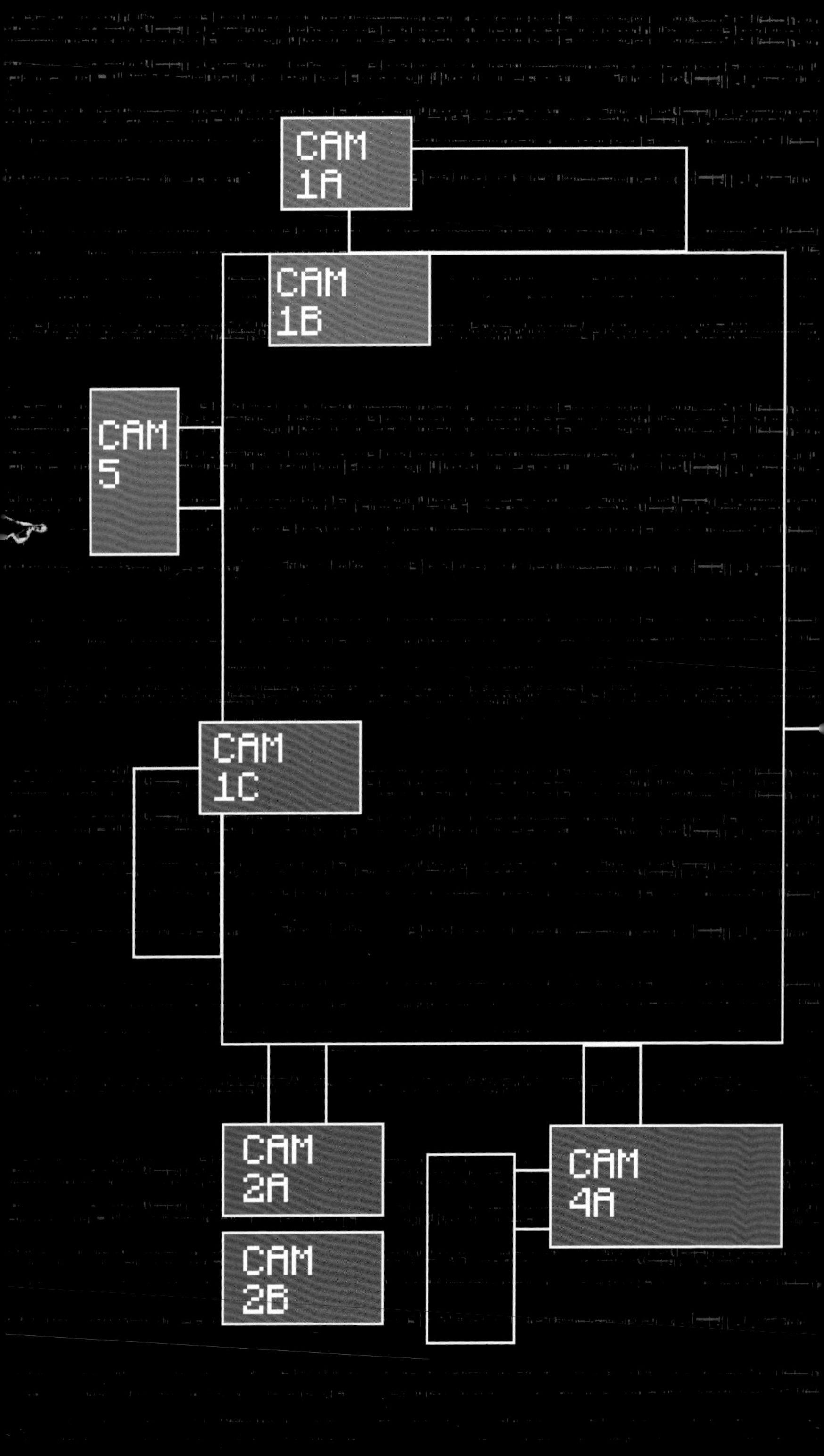
CAM 1A
CAM 1B
CAM 5
CAM 1C
CAM 2A
CAM 2B
CAM 4A

INTRODUCTION

In *Five Nights at Freddy's*, you play as a security guard patrolling Freddy Fazbear's Pizza.

IT'S HARD TO DENY THE LASTING IMPACT

that *Five Nights at Freddy's* has had on people over the last few years. With over nine installments in the main series and countless spin-offs, the franchise has grown to become a household name to many gamers and horror fans alike. The newest installment of the game, *Five Nights at Freddy's: Security Breach*, was one of the franchise's most anticipated games. With a free DLC slated to release in 2023, the hype for the franchise continues to grow.

Five Nights at Freddy's was first released in 2014 by creator Scott Cawthon, under his studio ScottGames. The game allows you to play as a newly hired security guard at Freddy Fazbear's Pizza. During the night shift, the animatronics begin to have a mind of their own and move around the building. You must utilize the security cameras, security doors, and electricity supply to remain vigilant and stay alive in this jumpscare, point-and-click horror game franchise. What started as a small self-contained indie game with simple mechanics has morphed into more elaborate releases on various platforms, including VR. Each release introduces something new and fresh, while still maintaining the series' most beloved features: spooky animatronics, eerie settings, and satisfying jumpscares.

So, what is it about this series that has dedicated fans coming back for more? The heart of *Five Nights at Freddy's* is truly its fan base. Experienced gamers, professionals, and influencers alike have taken to the game's delightfully scary lore. There are countless fan theories about the game's cryptic story, hidden secrets that are constantly being discovered, and fan art, videos, and cosplay that continue to remain popular for years after the game's initial release. Beyond the game itself, *Five Nights at Freddy's* has presented itself in various other forms of popular media that has increased its longevity and drawn even more fans into the frightening world Scott Cawthon created. Players can spot the iconic jumpscares in viral memes, as well as enjoy various fan arts and cosplays. We can only wait to see what other truths will be unraveled as the story continues and the franchise marches into the future.

You can't enjoy the full extent of this gaming series from playing the games alone. Cawthon has expertly hidden secrets and lore in game trailers, spin-offs, books, and promotional materials. But don't worry. We have unlocked all the best elements of the game for you. Read on for the history of the franchise, plus tips, tricks, and fun finds!

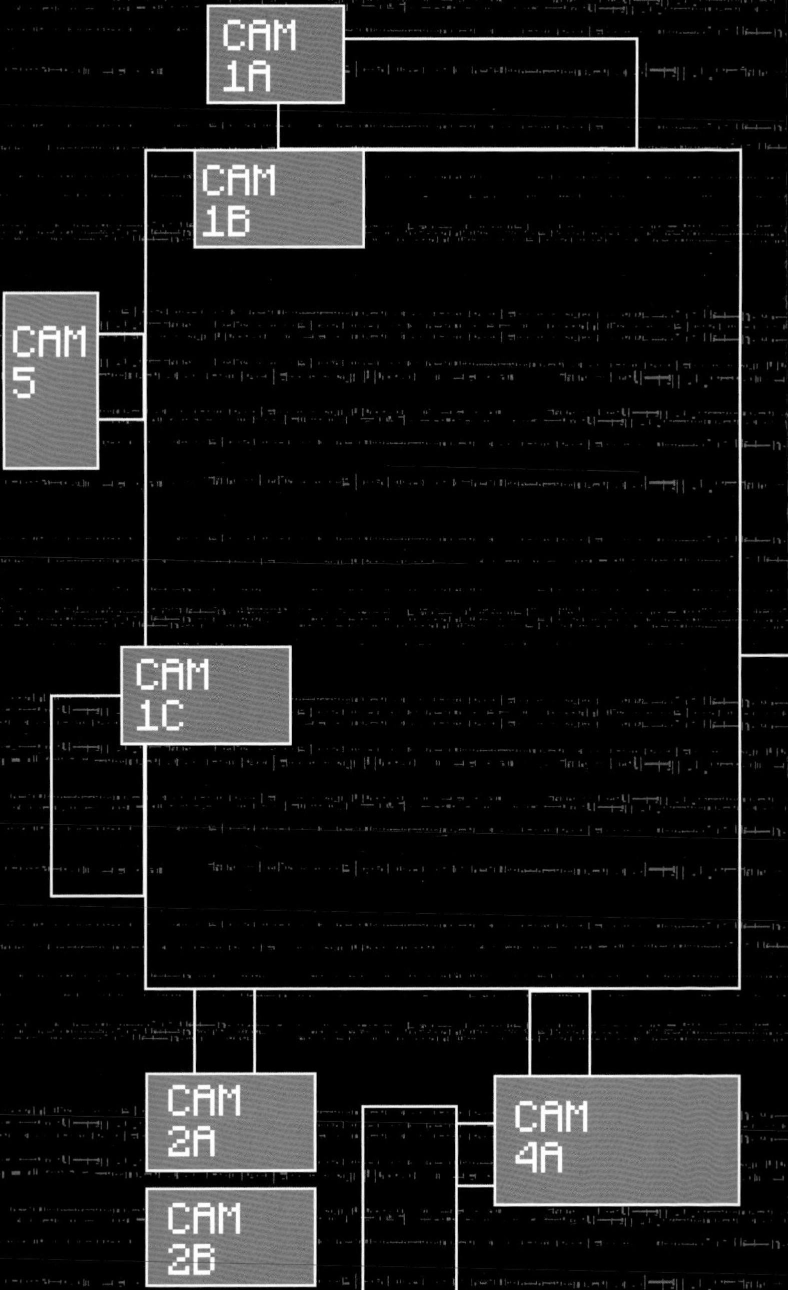
CAM 1A
CAM 1B
CAM 5
CAM 1C
CAM 2A
CAM 2B
CAM 4A

FIVE NIGHTS AT FREDDY'S:
THE ORIGINAL

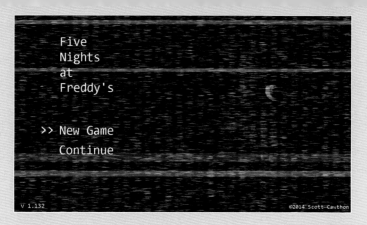

Five Nights at Freddy's is playable on the PC, Nintendo Switch, Playstation 4 and 5, Xbox One, the Xbox Series X/S, and Mobile.

On the title screen, players will have two options. They can either start a new game or continue from where they left off last. There is no settings menu and hitting the 'esc' key on the PC version will shut down the game immediately. There is no save game option, so players must complete a night before their progress is recorded.

Starting a new game will take the player to the beginning of the game's campaign, identifiable by a newspaper clipping of a help wanted ad. From there, players will meet the Phone Guy who will explain what the player's duty is as the new security guard. Clicking continue will take the player to the beginning of the night they last played.

The basic mechanics are simple and are the same on each platform. The player is given access to three things: a security camera monitor, light buttons, and door buttons. The player can reach the security monitor by clicking or selecting the bottom of the screen which has an arrow indicator. The security monitor shows eleven cameras that you can cycle through. Each one shows you a different area of Freddy Fazbear's Pizzeria. Players will use these cams to pinpoint where each animatronic is as the night goes on. Players also have access to two buttons that can lock the doors to the East and West Hall. This will prevent the animatronics from breaking into the office and attacking the player. The player can also use light buttons on either the West or East door to see any blind spots that the security cameras don't pick up. You'll need to use these lights if you can't pinpoint an animatronic's location on the map.

Power left: 83%
Usage:

Players can click or select the arrow at the bottom of their screen to access the security monitor. The buttons allow them to lock doors and turn on lights.

There is one caveat to these tools. Using either the buttons or the security monitor will drain power and running out of power will almost always end in game over. So, you'll want to be mindful of how much battery life is being depleted. You can tell this by looking at the lower left half of the screen which will give you a percentage. There is also an indicator marked "usage" that will show the player how many of their tools are being used currently.

Power left: 56%
Usage:

Check your power in the bottom left corner. The buttons and monitor will drain it quickly and put you at risk of an untimely demise.

» THE GOAL

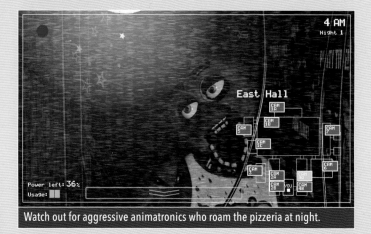

Watch out for aggressive animatronics who roam the pizzeria at night.

In *Five Nights at Freddy's*, the player's main goal is to survive six full nights at Freddy Fazbear's Pizzeria. The shift starts at 12 a.m. and ends at 6 a.m. Players must be mindful of the animatronics' locations, what sounds they're making, and the power supply percentage.

Some animatronics will move around quite a bit.

Players must sometimes rely on their sense of sound to locate where the animatronics have moved to. For example, clinking of pots and pans will tell players that Chica has walked off the stage and into the Kitchen. In this instance, you will not have to click around to find her, which will save you some power.

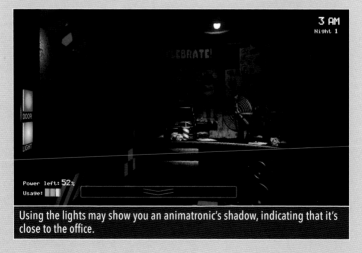

Using the lights may show you an animatronic's shadow, indicating that it's close to the office.

Keep your ears open for these sound effects:

POUNDING ON THE DOOR: Players will hear this sound when an animatronic is trying to get inside one of the Office's locked doors.

FOOTSTEPS: Footsteps can be heard when Freddy is moving around the pizzeria.

HUMMING: If you hear humming, it's most likely Foxy singing!

MUSIC BOX: If you hear this sound, it isn't a good sign. You must have run out of power! Freddy is coming.

EERIE MUSIC: Did the background music suddenly get more creepy? That's because one of the animatronics is approaching the Office.

STRAINED BREATHING: This sound plays if Bonnie or Chica is in the Office but the player has their security monitor up.

WHISPERING: You'll hear whispering when Freddy has snuck into the Office.

LAUGHING: If you hear laughing, it may mean that Golden Freddy has been summoned.

WARNING!

This game contains flashing lights, loud noises, and lots of jumpscares!

Make sure you're wearing headphones to contain the noise of this game!

» WHO IS FREDDY FAZBEAR?

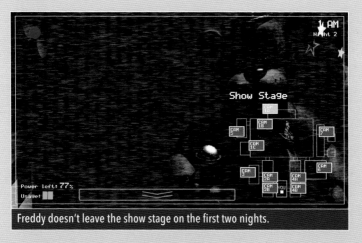

Freddy doesn't leave the show stage on the first two nights.

Freddy Fazbear is the main antagonist in Freddy Fazbear's Pizzeria. Along with his animatronic counterparts, Chica and Bonnie, he aims to attack any adults that may show up in the pizzeria after closing. Unfortunately, that includes you, so watch out!

At night time, Freddy can be heard taunting the player by laughing and often playing a song right before he is about to pounce. So if you hear music, the end could be near. Overall, Freddy Fazbear is mischievous and sneaky, so don't assume you know where he is in the game or what he's up to.

FAZBEAR FACT: IN THE ORIGINAL *FIVE NIGHTS AT FREDDY'S* GAME, FREDDY WAS ONLY MEANT TO INTERACT WITH THE PLAYER IF THEY'D RUN OUT OF POWER. THIS WAS CHANGED IN THE FINAL VERSION OF THE GAME, WHERE HE ACTIVATES ON NIGHT 3.

» WHO IS CHICA?

Chica will look into the security camera to taunt you.

Similar to Freddy Fazbear, Chica is another animatronic to keep your eye on. She wears a bib that reads "Let's Eat!!!" and can be most often found in the kitchen area of the Pizzeria after-hours. She carries around a cupcake that acts as if it has a mind of its own.

Chica loves pizza, which can work to your advantage in the game. At times, she's so distracted by her pizza obsession that she'll head to the kitchen to hunt down food instead of going after you! She can also be considered stubborn and a bit determined, so it's not unusual for her to stay outside the security door's entrance the longest.

FAZBEAR FACT: CHICA IS THE ONLY ANIMATRONIC FROM *FIVE NIGHTS AT FREDDY'S* THAT APPEARS IN ANOTHER FRANCHISE. SHE SHOWS UP IN THE GAME *CREEPY CASTLE*, DEVELOPED BY DOPTERRA. SCOTT CAWTHON DONATED TO THE GAME'S KICKSTARTER AND OFFERED UP CHICA AS A PLAYABLE CHARACTER!

» WHO IS BONNIE?

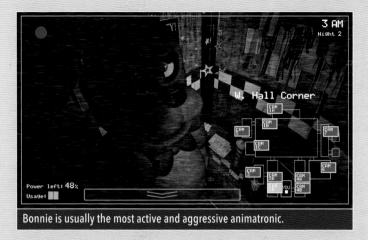

Bonnie is usually the most active and aggressive animatronic.

Bonnie is the third animatronic member of Freddy Fazbear's band to have the ability to come to life and hunt you down at night. You'll notice that Bonnie is usually the first animatronic to leave his spot on the stage during the night shift. He seems to be more aggressive than his other animatronic companions, so you'll want to be ready for him.

Bonnie will sometimes try to trick a player by not going his usual route, so don't let him catch you off guard. However, while he attacks most often and seems to play the dirtiest, Bonnie will leave the security entrance quicker than the other animatronics. You can often find him gazing directly at the security cameras as if he knows you're watching him. Don't let him intimidate you. You've got this!

FAZBEAR FACT: SCOTT CAWTHON THINKS THAT BONNIE IS THE SCARIEST OF ALL THE ANIMATRONICS. HE CLAIMS THAT BONNIE EVEN GAVE HIM NIGHTMARES WHILE CODING HIM INTO THE GAME!

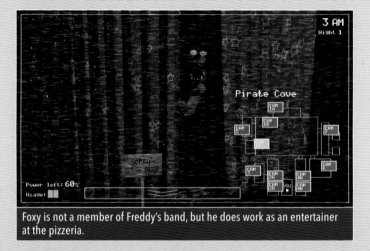

Foxy is not a member of Freddy's band, but he does work as an entertainer at the pizzeria.

Foxy, an animatronic pirate entertainer at Freddy Fazbear's Pizzeria, acts as a secondary antagonist in the original *Five Nights at Freddy's* game. While he isn't always front and center, look for Foxy creeping around the pizzeria, ready to pounce in a moment's notice. The pirate animatronic is hard to trick and he remains vigilant, so beware of him as you navigate your security job!

GAMEPLAY TIP: Foxy isn't usually active on the first night, but once in a while he will be.

» FREDDY FAZBEAR'S PIZZERIA

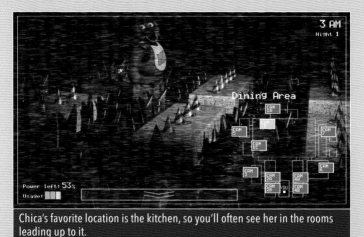

Chica's favorite location is the kitchen, so you'll often see her in the rooms leading up to it.

The first *Five Nights at Freddy's* game takes place at one of the restaurants in the fictional pizzeria chain, Freddy Fazbear's Pizza during the early 1990s. This pizza place is supposed to be a family friendly establishment modeled after popular dine-and-play restaurants like Chuck E. Cheese and Showbiz Pizza Place. Parents and their children are welcomed to the restaurant to eat dinner or throw a party while they watch Freddy's animatronic band play music. In the morning, everything plays out as innocently as it sounds. At night, however, things take a dark and twisted turn.

There are a total of 10 areas to be aware of in Freddy Fazbear's Pizzeria, all of which can be seen on the security cameras. The first area is the office where the player will start and physically remain. You may be able to see the other spaces on the security cameras but you will not be able to leave the office to visit them. In fact, your goal is to keep the animatronics out of the office so that you can survive the night!

Upon first entering the small space, you'll notice a few key things. On the wall there's a poster with Freddy and the band that reads "CELEBRATE!" To the right of that is a few childlike drawings of the animatronics plastered on the wall behind a desk fan. When you start the game, the person who presumably hired you calls you to give advice and informs you of what the night will entail. Listen closely to his words as he provides a bit of lore as well as tips on how to play the game.

FAZBEAR FACT: DID YOU KNOW THAT THE "PHONE GUY" IS ACTUALLY VOICED BY THE *FIVE NIGHTS AT FREDDY'S* CREATOR, SCOTT CAWTHON?

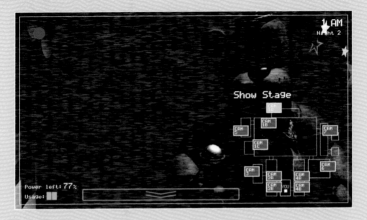

The show stage is where Freddy, Chica, and Bonnie perform their tunes during the day time. At nighttime, this is where the animatronics are left deactivated. According to the phone guy, these animatronics have been left in free roam mode at night because of "Something about their servos locking up if they get turned off for too long." So, you may notice on your security cameras that some, or even all of, Freddy's band may be missing. When an animatronic leaves the stage, the others may change their position or direction in which they are looking. In very rare occurrences you can catch Freddy looking directly at the camera.

GAMEPLAY TIP: The Show Stage is where the security camera will automatically default to. When an animatronic leaves the stage, it will not come back until the next night. So, to avoid losing extra power and time, you can skip checking the stage in this instance. You can also avoid checking the stage if only Freddy is present on the first two nights as he will not leave until the third.

The backstage area is meant to be a place for employees to repair the animatronics during the day shift.

The backstage area is to the left of the Show Stage on the security camera map. It is identifiable by the checkered floors and dismembered animatronic parts. This area is meant to be where the animatronics can be repaired during the daytime if they break. The only animatronic that will enter this room during the night time is Bonnie.

FAZBEAR FACT: THE IN-GAME MODEL USED FOR FREDDY FAZBEAR'S SPARE HEAD IS DIFFERENT FROM THE ONE USED ON THE ACTUAL FREDDY ANIMATRONIC THAT RESIDES ON THE STAGE.

» DINING AREA

A shadowy figure of Chica can be seen peering into the camera.

Directly in front of the Show Stage is the Dining Area. In the daytime this is where patrons of Freddy Fazbear's Pizzeria sit to watch the band perform. There are six tables set up with party hats and confetti which insinuates that many parties are held in this room. This is the largest area that can be seen on the security cameras. As this space is right next to the show stage, you'll want to keep an eye on it as Bonnie, Chica, and Freddy will pass through it to get to the Office. There is a light shining in the middle of the dining area, though no other areas can be seen clearly in the dark.

» RESTROOMS

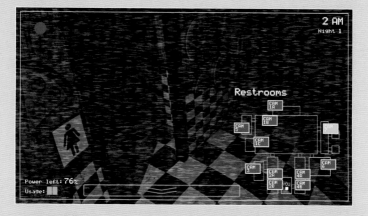

The restrooms are located to the right of the dining area. From the security camera, you will be able to see doors leading to the female and male bathrooms respectively. There are pizza decorations on the walls. Both Freddy and Chica can appear in this area.

GAMEPLAY TIP: If you're looking for Freddy in this area, keep your eyes focused in or near the Women's bathroom, not the Men's.

The message on the sign in Pirate's Cove can change, so keep an eye on it!

Pirate Cove shows up to the left of the dining area and next to the backstage area. There is a sign that reads "Sorry! Out of Order." The man on the phone informs the player to keep an eye on the curtains in this room. He says, "The character in there seems unique in that he becomes more active if the cameras remain off for long periods of time." You can sometimes see Foxy poking his head out of the purple curtains that block the pirate attraction from view. This will happen if, as the phone guy says, the cameras are off of the room for prolonged periods of time. If left for too long, Foxy can leave the stage and run towards the player, ending in a game over.

FAZBEAR FACT: THE SIGN IN FRONT OF PIRATE COVE CAN SOMETIMES CHANGE TO "IT'S ME!" SO KEEP AN EYE ON IT AS YOU CLICK THROUGH THE CAMS!

The kitchen cams are blocked out, but sometimes you can hear Chica playing around in there.

The kitchen is unique in the fact that the camera feed is disabled in this area. Upon clicking this camera, players will be met with a black screen that has an error message, "Camera disabled. Audio only." Though you can't see her, you'll often hear Chica rummaging around in the kitchen, clanging pots and pans. This sound effect can be heard even if the camera isn't set to the kitchen area. Freddy is also able to visit the kitchen which can be determined by the sound of his jingle being played near the room. Bonnie and Foxy will never cross through the kitchen, so players can rest easy.

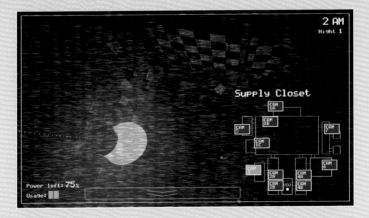

There is not a lot going on in the supply closet, at least upon first glance. A shelf sits on the wall across from the door. A mop can be seen as well with a crumpled up piece of paper next to it. The security camera in this room is on top of the ceiling rather than on the walls, so you get an overhead view. This camera also remains still, not moving left or right like the others. The supply closet will only be visited by Bonnie. As such, there are only two views of the room you can get: one with or without Bonnie standing in it!

GAMEPLAY TIP: The Supply Closet is a room seldom visited by the animatronics. Because of this, it's a good idea to avoid checking this camera as a way to save power.

FAZBEAR FACT: THE SUPPLY CLOSET HAS BLUE TILES, WHILE THE EAST AND WEST HALLS FEATURE RED TILES.

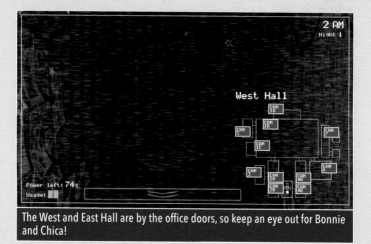

The West and East Hall are by the office doors, so keep an eye out for Bonnie and Chica!

The West and East Hall are on either side of the office. The West Hall also connects to the supply closet. In this area, there is a checkered floor and hand-drawn images of the animatronics on the wall. It is on this side that Bonnie and Foxy will try and reach the office to attack the player. In certain cases, like if the power is out, Freddy will use the West Hall, though this action is not picked up on the security camera. In the West Hall, the lights will flicker on and off. Bonnie will only be visible if the lights are on him. The player will be able to turn on the hall light from the office and in doing so will be able to see Bonnie standing outside of the door. On and after Night 4, Bonnie can be seen in the corner of the hall with his head twitching. An audio file will help players identify if Bonnie is in the corner, eliminating the need to use power to check the area. Foxy can run at the player if they are looking at the West Hall on their security monitor.

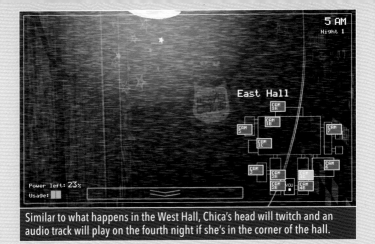

Similar to what happens in the West Hall, Chica's head will twitch and an audio track will play on the fourth night if she's in the corner of the hall.

Chica and Freddy will use the East Hall to reach the office. On one of the walls is a poster with the restaurant rules but this can sometimes change to newspaper clippings. If Freddy is spotted in the corner of the East Hall it means he is close to attacking you. You must close the right door before switching cams or he will try and kill you.

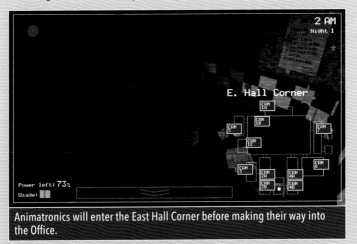

Animatronics will enter the East Hall Corner before making their way into the Office.

EASTER EGG ALERT: GOLDEN FREDDY

You can summon a fourth hidden animatronic known as Golden Freddy by using the cam in the West Hall. This can happen on any night but is most common on Night 1 and less likely to happen on Night 3. To activate this event, you'll need to start at Cam 2B and look at the poster on the wall. The design will normally be of Freddy holding a microphone with the word "Celebrate!" on it. It can also rarely show the image of Freddy trying to rip his own head off. This is believed by many fans to be the spirit inside of Freddy trying to escape the robotic skeleton.

If you see the image of Golden Freddy in place of the other posters, it means you have summoned him and will see his corpse inside the Office once you put the cam monitor away. To get to this point, you'll need to keep switching between Cam 2B and other cams. Once you see the Golden Freddy poster, you need to close the monitor before switching to another. You have a few seconds to pull the cams back up before a Golden Freddy jumpscare pops up and your game force closes. Your game will not close if Golden Freddy pops up on Night 3.

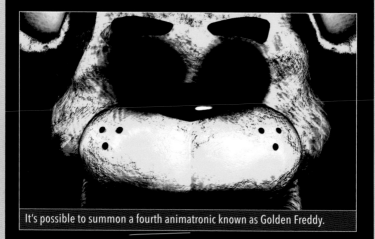

It's possible to summon a fourth animatronic known as Golden Freddy.

» NIGHT 1

12:00 AM
1st Night

The first night is the easiest, but it may still pose a challenge to inexperienced players.

Night 1 is by far the easiest to survive. This is because the animatronics aren't extremely active. Freddy Fazbear will not awaken until Night 3. The only exception is if the power is fully depleted. Foxy is also very unlikely to wake up and leave Pirate Cove. Bonnie is the most active of the four animatronics, but he does not leave the stage until 2 a.m. Chica will not become active until an hour later, at 3 a.m.

Because of this, you will have an easy time exploring the pizzeria by using the security camera monitor. Be mindful of the power supply, which will always tick down even if you aren't actively using the security monitor, door locks, or lights.

Once the game starts, the player should let the message on the phone play fully before opening up the security monitor. This will help conserve power. From here, you'll be able to explore the rooms. Be sure to check the Show Stage to see whether any animatronic has left to roam the pizzeria.

You can use the East and West lights more often in this stage in place of the security monitor. Do this after 2 a.m., when Bonnie awakens. In later nights when Freddy and Foxy are more active, this will not be the ideal strategy, as it'll leave you with blind spots and deplete the power too quickly.

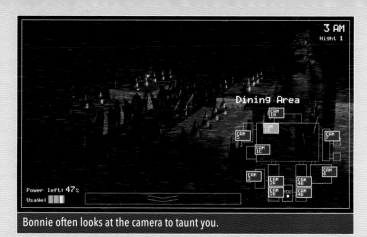

Bonnie often looks at the camera to taunt you.

However, on day one this works well because you only need to prevent Bonnie and Chica from entering the Office. Rather than clicking around the security monitors to see where each animatronic is, you'll save time and energy by focusing in on the two hallways and their lights.

Do not keep the lights on the entire time. You'll waste too much energy and trigger a game over. Instead, alternate the lights every so often, especially if you see the animatronics in a specific hall. You can also tell whether an animatronic is approaching the Office by looking at the security cameras in the East and West Halls.

If an animatronic is by the window of the office, make sure the door is closed so they can't break in!

If Bonnie is blocking the normal path of light in the West Hall, he's close to the Office. This is similar to Chica, but on the East side of the Office. If you spot Bonnie or Chica while using the hall lights, you want to close the respective door immediately. Any delay could cause a door jam.

» WHAT IS A DOOR JAM?

Be careful! Sometimes doors can jam.

If a door jams, that means an animatronic has entered your Office and you can no longer close the door on them. Pulling up your security monitor and exiting the cams will result in a jumpscare and instant game over. Bonnie and Chica are also able to pull down your monitor screen, so be careful. If you'd like to survive while your door is jammed, you'll need to wait it out. This isn't a guaranteed strategy and will likely only work the closer you are to 6 a.m.

GAMEPLAY TIP: If you'd like a surefire way of winning Night 1, the easiest thing to do is close the West Hall door at 2 a.m., when Bonnie awakens. He'll only enter the Office from that side. Chica will most likely not make it to the Office before the night ends, so Bonnie will be your biggest threat.

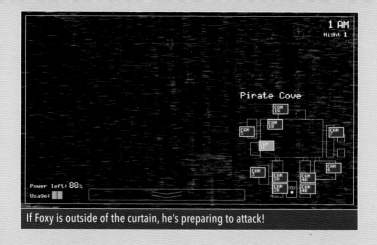

Pirate Cove

Power left: 88%
Usage: ▮▮

If Foxy is outside of the curtain, he's preparing to attack!

GAMEPLAY TIP: While you don't have to do it often, checking Pirate Cove will prevent Foxy from attacking, as he only becomes active when there is no one watching. In rare instances, you can trigger the Golden Freddy animatronic, which will result in death if you do not pull up your security monitor right away.

FAZBEAR FACT: IN THE GAME *HELP WANTED*, IT'S REVEALED THAT FOXY WAS ORIGINALLY CALLED CAPTAIN FOXY. HE EVEN WORE A PIRATE SUIT, INCLUDING A JACKET, HAT, AND EYE PATCH. THAT MODEL WAS DISCONTINUED AND REPLACED WITH THE ONE WE SEE IN THE FIRST *FIVE NIGHT'S AT FREDDY'S* GAME.

12:00 AM
2nd Night

Each night will start at 12:00 a.m.

The nights get progressively harder as the game goes on. You should again listen to the full phone call before opening up your security monitors and clicking around. This is to save as much energy as possible. Checking the Show Stage and Pirate Cove should be your top priority at this stage. Looking at the Show Stage will tell you whether Bonnie or Chica have become active yet. Freddy will not begin moving around until Night 3.

GAMEPLAY TIP: The trick to surviving this night is being fast. You'll want to be able to close doors, open lights, and flick the security camera up and down rather quickly to avoid being attacked and jumpscared.

Remember that Bonnie will only come to the Office from the West Hall and Chica will only enter the Office from the East Hall. The latter is much slower and easier to contain. Bonnie is more difficult to keep track of, but keeping an eye on the West side cams and lights will help. Be sure to close the left door if you catch sight of Bonnie in the West Hall or if you see him when using the lights.

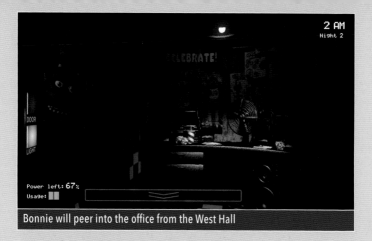

Power left: 67%
Usage:

Bonnie will peer into the office from the West Hall

The animatronic in Pirate Cove, Foxy, will become more active the less the camera is on him. Foxy's attacks are much quicker and more sudden than those of Bonnie and Chica. If Foxy feels like no one is watching, he'll dash from behind the purple curtains of Pirate Cove and barrel toward the Office. You will be able to see Foxy running on the cameras and hear his screams. You'll need to be extremely quick to stop him from reaching the Office and attacking you.

GAMEPLAY TIP: When Foxy begins to bang on the Office doors, he will not be able to get in, but will sap some power as he does so.

» HOW TO STOP FOXY

Foxy will normally peer outside of the purple curtains in Pirate Cove. As long as you see him there, you should be fine. However, if you see Foxy standing outside of the curtains with his head tilted back, it means he is preparing to jet toward the Office. Changing the cams to the West Hall will show you this.

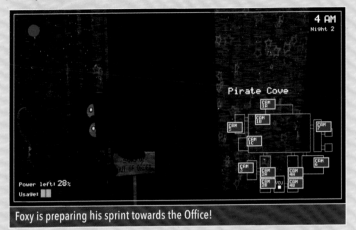

Foxy is preparing his sprint towards the Office!

The easiest way to stop Foxy is to lower the monitor and close the left door when you see he is no longer in Pirate Cove. He will only run through the West Hall, which makes things slightly easier. However, going about it this way will cost you more power. The first time you successfully block foxy you will lose 1 percent of battery, 7 percent on the second block, and 6 percent on each subsequent block. While effective, this strategy may drain too much of your power source.

An even better and more proactive way to rid yourself of Foxy is to make sure he never leaves Pirate Cove at all. You can check any camera, not just the one in Pirate Cove, to keep Foxy at bay. Doing so every few seconds will show you where the other animatronics are as well.

GAMEPLAY TIP: Keep in mind that Foxy cannot be detected using the hall lights.

12:00 AM
3rd Night

On Night 3, things will begin to get more difficult.

Freddy Fazbear will finally leave the Show Stage on this night, making the game even more difficult. You'll want to keep in mind the previous tips about stopping Foxy, Bonnie, and Chica. However, keep in mind that Chica will leave the Show Stage earlier than Bonnie on this night and will be more aggressive than usual. Bonnie won't maneuver off the Show Stage until 2 or 3 a.m.

On this night you should focus your efforts on pinpointing Freddy's location using the security camera. Use the left and right hall lights as you did on Night 1 if you want to check on Bonnie and Chica. Make sure that you're using the security camera frequently enough that you don't activate Foxy's sprint but also not so much that you deplete your power level too quickly.

» HOW TO STOP FREDDY

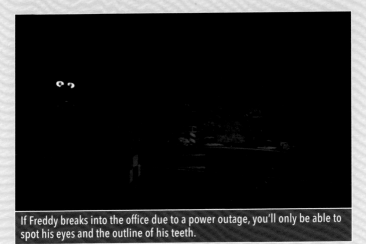

If Freddy breaks into the office due to a power outage, you'll only be able to spot his eyes and the outline of his teeth.

Freddy has a set path that he travels on every night after he awakens. Once Freddy steps off the Show Stage, he'll make his way over to the Dining Area. From there, he'll go to the Restrooms. He will only travel to the Kitchen after the Restrooms. There's no camera feed in the Kitchen, so you'll need to listen for Freddy's theme song, which will alert you to his presence there. Just like Chica, Freddy will enter the Office from the East. He'll travel through the East Hall and end up in the East Hall Corner. You'll be able to spot Freddy quite easily in any of these rooms by his glowing white eyes.

If you see Freddy in the East Hall Corner, you must close the door so that he can't enter the Office. If you hear his laughter and the door is open, chances are that Freddy is in the Office and it's game over. If you successfully lock Freddy out of the Office, he'll go to another room and continue the pattern described above.

You can also tell which location Freddy is going to by the number of laughs you hear as he moves around the pizzeria. If you hear one laugh, he's in the dining room. If you hear two laughs, Freddy is in the Restrooms. Three laughs signify that he's in the Kitchen; he'll have laughed four times by the time he's in the East Hall and five times when he's in the East Hall Corner. If he's in the East Hall Corner and laughs a sixth time, he has left the East Hall Corner and you can open the door.

There is only a small chance of Freddy attacking on Night 3.

GAMEPLAY TIP: If you can see Freddy in the East Hall Corner, he will not be able to get into the Office while the camera is on him. This is because Freddy cannot sneak into the Office like Bonnie and Chica can. He'll only be able to get in if you have the security monitor up.

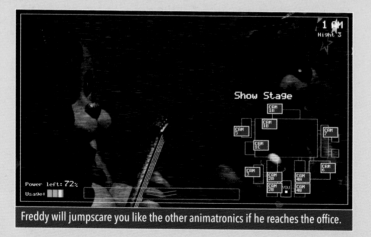

Freddy will jumpscare you like the other animatronics if he reaches the office.

The last few nights are the most difficult of the game. You'll need to be vigilant and know where each animatronic is. Use your ears, eyes, and tools to help you fend off the wrath of Freddy, Chica, Bonnie, and Foxy.

» NIGHT 4

Prepare for a challenge on Night 4.

Night 4 can be particularly difficult because all the animatronics are active and likely moving around. Also, the amount of power that drains from using your tools has increased. Freddy can either be as active as he was the night before or even more active, which will be randomly determined at the start of the round. Therefore, he is your wildcard and despite knowing his pattern, he will be hard to predict.

Freddy will only move around if you are not watching him. You should keep an eye on him while he's on the Show Stage to prolong his time there. When or if Freddy decides to move, be sure to check his new location on the security cameras, as this will slow down his movement and keep him in his current area for a longer time. Be sure to also check up on Foxy in Pirate Cove to make sure he hasn't left the area.

Chica will likely be the first animatronic to move. Both she and Bonnie have a high chance of being gone from the Show Stage by the time the player first checks the security monitor. Unlike on the other nights, Bonnie and Chica's heads will begin to twitch and a sound can be heard coming from them if they are in the West and East Hall Corners, respectively. This sound can be heard directly from the Office without having to pull the security monitor up. This will allow you to pinpoint their location without having to search on the cams, which will ultimately preserve some power.

Chica will deliver a frightening jumpscare!

Bonnie will still only enter the Office from the West side and Chica from the East side. Therefore, if you hear a robotic noise coming from either side of the Office, you should turn on the lights and check for Bonnie or Chica's appearance. If you see them, be sure to close the Office doors to block them out.

Beware of an attack from Bonnie.

Chica and Bonnie can still jam the doors on this night. The lights and doors will become disabled if you fail to keep an eye on the two animatronics as they maneuver around the pizzeria. In this instance, the doors and lights will not turn back on, leaving you vulnerable to animatronic attacks. This will be hard to overcome, so try avoiding it altogether. However, if you find yourself stuck in this situation, you'll want to avoid pulling up the security cameras because pulling them back down can trigger an attack. If you're not close to 6 a.m., this may almost be a guaranteed death sentence.

Foxy will stick his body into the office before initiating a jumpscare.

You want to focus on checking the Show Stage and Pirate Cove this round to slow down Freddy and Foxy's movements. If you continually check the Show Stage, there is a chance Freddy won't move from it at all. To keep Foxy from getting out of the purple curtain and leaving Pirate Cove, you'll want to check the area on the cams about six times per hour.

So, a worthwhile strategy would be to first check the lights and then Pirate Cove. Do it again, but this time also check the Show Stage. If you check Pirate Cove and the purple curtain is open, make sure you lower the security monitor and lock the left door. Clicking the West Hall on the security monitor will give you less time to save yourself from Foxy's attack.

FAZBEAR FACT: IT IS ON NIGHT 4 THAT PHONE GUY GIVES YOU YOUR LAST MESSAGE. HE TELLS THE PLAYER TO CHECK THE SUITS IN THE BACK ROOM BEFORE YOU HEAR BANGING ON THE DOOR AND GARBLED ANIMATRONIC NOISES. THIS SUGGESTS THAT HE WAS KILLED AND STUFFED INSIDE ONE OF THE EMPTY ANIMATRONIC SHELLS IN THE BACKSTAGE AREA.

12:00 AM
5th Night

Night 5 is one of the most difficult nights to beat.

Be on guard on Night 5, as the animatronics are extremely active. The amount of power depleted is also exponentially increased. Keep in mind all of the tips from the other nights. Foxy will still leave Pirate Cove if you do not check the camera often enough. Freddy follows the same path, but he moves around more frequently. Similarly, as we've suggested before, you want to use the lights to check whether Bonnie and Chica are close to the Office. This will save energy.

If you suspect they've entered the Office while you were distracted, do not pull up the security monitor. However, in this case, you run the risk of triggering Foxy's run toward the Office. A good strategy to complete this night is to click on the cam for Pirate Cove first. Make sure that the East door is closed so that Freddy cannot enter the Office. Then, you'll want to check the lights on both doors to see whether Bonnie or Chica is nearby. You can continually repeat this process until the night is over. Be mindful of how much power you are using throughout this process, as hitting zero means game over.

Another strategy that may work is to check the Show Stage often. You want to make sure you check the lights first to keep an eye on Chica and Bonnie. Doing this will cause Freddy to stay in position and not walk around the pizzeria. You still have to be mindful of Foxy, so make sure you're checking Pirate Cove as well. When using the camera, you want to be as quick as possible so as not to waste any energy.

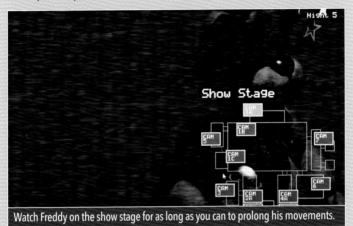

Watch Freddy on the show stage for as long as you can to prolong his movements.

Losing power by closing the door on Foxy will be detrimental and probably cause a game over. Therefore, your main goal should be keeping him in Pirate Cove and Freddy on stage. Do not forget to continually check the lights for Bonnie and Chica. If you see them, be sure to close their respective doors.

If Freddy leaves the stage, you have to check the East Hall Corner. If he is in that room, do not lower the camera. Watching him will keep him in place until he moves to another room. If you do lower the camera, he will sneak into the Office and attack you. You can also avoid using the security camera to check for Freddy by counting his laughs. If you hear the fifth laugh, close the East door. When Freddy laughs again, that means he has moved away from the East Hall. Check for him and Chica first on the monitor before opening the door again.

6 AM

At 6 a.m. on Night 5, you will have officially beaten the game's main campaign.

After you complete the fifth night, you have successfully beaten *Five Nights at Freddy's*. You will be given your paycheck and will eventually return to the game's title screen. On the title screen you'll notice a new option is available under "Continue." You will now be able to play through a secret bonus night (Night 6).

FAZBEAR FACT: IT IS ON NIGHT 5 WHERE YOU LEARN THE PROTAGONIST'S NAME IS MIKE SCHMIDT. IT IS LABELED ON THE CHECK HE RECEIVES.

If you choose the continue option, you'll be brought to the beginning of the bonus night, which is also called Night 6.

You'll earn $120.50 for completing your shift on the sixth night.

12:00 AM
6th Night

Night 6 is a bonus night you can unlock if you complete the game's main story.

Night 6 is the hardest night to beat in *Five Nights at Freddy's*. All of the animatronics are even more active than the night before. You can follow an identical strategy to Night 5, but you may need to adjust some things to accommodate the new difficulty level.

A popular strategy among many *Five Nights at Freddy's* players is checking the Show Stage at the beginning of the night. Afterward, you'll pull the security monitor down and do it again. Then, you'll check on the left and right lights to make sure that Bonnie and Chica are not there. You'll want to keep repeating this process until you either run out of power or eventually win the night.

To minimize the amount of power you use, you need to check the security camera as quickly as possible. Spending extra time on this step will use unnecessary power. This strategy works for many players because it renders two of the four animatronics frozen in their spots.

By checking the Show Stage constantly, you'll be preventing Freddy from leaving. That means you won't need to click around the security monitor and waste more power. This action will also keep Foxy at bay. You need to check the camera a certain number of times an hour to make sure that Foxy doesn't leave Pirate Cove. On Night 6, you will need to trust that, without checking Pirate Cove to confirm, Foxy has not left the area. By checking Pirate Cove for Foxy, you run the risk of wasting unnecessary power; checking the Show Stage is more effective in keeping Freddy in his place. Do not forget to use the hall lights to check for Bonnie and Chica, as they will be extremely active, showing up more than usual.

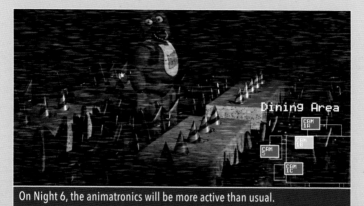

On Night 6, the animatronics will be more active than usual.

FAZBEAR FACT: YOU WILL RECEIVE NO PHONE MESSAGES ON NIGHT 6.

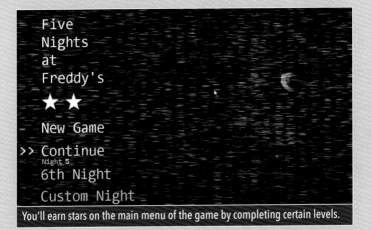

You'll earn stars on the main menu of the game by completing certain levels.

Once you beat Night 6, Mike Schmidt is given a check for $120.50. This unlocks the custom night, which is also known as the seventh night. This game mode allows you to change the level of the animatronics.

Setting Freddy's level to one or two will make him inactive. Setting his level to three, four, five, or six will cause him to act as he does on Night 3. He will move even more if you have his level set anywhere from seven to twelve.

GAMEPLAY TIP: To get Freddy's most active levels, you'll want to set his numbers anywhere from thirteen to twenty. This makes it very likely he will strike the Office!

By setting Bonnie and Chica's level to one or two, they'll be as active as they were on Night 2. Raising the level will make them appear more often. Higher levels will also make it easier for Bonnie and Chica to disable the doors and lights. The animatronics will also give you less time to close the doors and prevent them from entering the Office.

The number you set Foxy's level to affects how often he appears, how easy it is for him to attack, and how fast he rushes to the Office. The higher the number, the harder it will be to defeat Foxy. Set his numbers anywhere from three to six to get his behavior from Night 3. For an added challenge, set his level from seven to twelve.

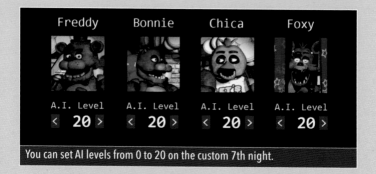

12:00 AM

7th Night

There is another secret bonus night that the player can unlock by completing six nights.

FAZBEAR FACT: THE EXTRA FIFTY CENTS MIKE EARNS ON HIS CHECK THIS NIGHT IS CREDITED TO OVERTIME.

Freddy	Bonnie	Chica	Foxy
A.I. Level	A.I. Level	A.I. Level	A.I. Level
< 20 >	< 20 >	< 20 >	< 20 >

You can set AI levels from 0 to 20 on the custom 7th night.

EASTER EGG ALERT: FUN CUSTOM NIGHT LEVELS

While you're free to put whatever numbers you'd like, here are some fun custom night modes to try out!

1/9/8/7

By entering these levels for each animatronic, you'll trigger Golden Freddy's appearance. This will work just like finding him in the regular five nights. Golden Freddy will appear and force close the main menu.

FAZBEAR FACT: THIS WAS ADDED BY SCOTT CAWTHON AS A JOKE TO ADDRESS A FAN RUMOR THAT THESE NUMBERS CAUSED A SECRET ENDING.

20/20/20/20

This mode is very challenging. You must set each animatronic to level twenty. As you'd expect, the animatronics are extraordinarily active. It will be difficult to ward off Foxy and Freddy! Be prepared for a challenge of the highest difficulty.

A common strategy used by players to complete this night is checking the East Hall Corner for Freddy, as this will prevent him from moving for a bit if you see him. Then, you'll check the lights and repeat.

Players have also chosen to only look at Pirate Cove on the security monitor. First, they activate the lights to check for Bonnie and Chica. Then, they close the right door to avoid being attacked by Freddy and pull up the monitor again to look at Pirate Cove. If you see that Foxy is gone, you'll want to quickly close the left door. After Foxy bangs on the door a few times he'll leave and you can open the left door and start again.

EASTER EGG ALERT:
FUN CUSTOM NIGHT LEVELS (CONTINUED)

FAZBEAR FACT: COMPLETING THIS CHALLENGE WILL EARN YOU AN EXTRA THIRD STAR ON THE MAIN MENU. YOUTUBERS MARKIPLIER AND BIGBUGZ WERE THE FIRST TO COMPLETE THIS EXCEPTIONALLY HARD MODE. SCOTT CAWTHON CREDITS THE LACK OF SPECIAL ENDING FOR COMPLETING THIS MODE TO THE FACT THAT HE HONESTLY BELIEVED IT WASN'T POSSIBLE TO COMPLETE.

0/0/0/0
This mode is the opposite of 20/20/20/20. It sets the animatronics to their lowest possible level. Beating this night will be a walk in the park.

FAZBEAR FACT: AFTER HAVING BEATEN THE SEVENTH NIGHT ON ANY MODE, YOU'LL BE GIVEN A NOTICE OF TERMINATION FOR "TAMPERING WITH THE ANIMATRONICS, GENERAL UNPROFESSIONALISM, AND ODOR." THIS IS THE LAST UNLOCKABLE LEVEL IN THE ORIGINAL *FIVE NIGHTS AT FREDDY'S*!

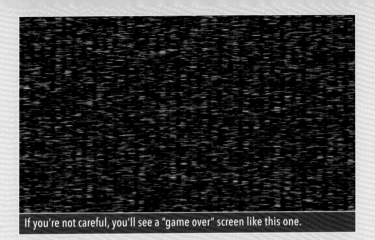
If you're not careful, you'll see a "game over" screen like this one.

There are a few ways that you can reach a game-over screen. As mentioned earlier, one way is to summon Golden Freddy, who will force close your game.

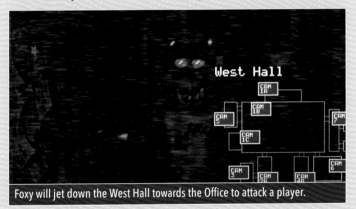
Foxy will jet down the West Hall towards the Office to attack a player.

Another way is if the power reaches 0 percent. In this instance, the Office will turn completely dark and any doors that were previously closed will spring open. You will not be able to close them again or access your security monitor. You'll see Freddy's glowing eyes and teeth flickering in the darkness. A music box version of his jingle will play and Freddy will jumpscare you.

You can reach a game-over screen if one of the animatronics sneaks into your Office. If you look at your security monitor when an animatronic is hiding in your Office, when you pull down the monitor, you'll be jumpscared.

Foxy can also attack you by running into your Office from Pirate Cove. If you do not look at your security monitor enough, this outcome will trigger.

The last way to reach a game-over screen is to . . . beat the game!

If you lose the game, the player is implied to have been stuffed inside a Freddy Fazbear suit.

» You'll want to use headphones. The game's audio will help you track down the animatronics, so you want to make sure you're able to hear the game clearly. Playing in complete silence, or with no background noise, will also keep you fully immersed.

» Listen for audio cues first before opening up the security monitor.

» The doors waste the most power in the game. You only want to use them when you know an animatronic is approaching the Office.

» Similarly, do not keep the lights on the entire game. Only keep them on for a few seconds as you check for Bonnie and Chica's locations.

» When you check the security monitor in later nights, you want to flick it up quickly. Staying on any given camera for a long time will sap your power.

» Keep an eye on the time in the top right-hand corner of the screen. Make sure you are not using too much power in the beginning of the night.

» Do not be afraid to restart a level in the middle of it. Doing so will save you some time (and maybe a headache!) in the long run.

» Freddy is hard to see in the dark. You'll be able to tell he's in a room by looking for his glowing eyes.

» The console version of *Five Nights at Freddy's* has cheats enabled. You can set unlimited power, which will make it so none of the power is depleted. You can enable a radar map, which will track animatronics on the cams for you. You can also set faster nights to make the night shorter. You can use these settings to help you practice before taking on a particularly tough night.

Good job, sport!
(see you next week)

			0123
		DATE 11-12-XX	
PAY TO THE ORDER OF Mike Schmidt		$ 130.00	
One Hundred twenty dollars		DOLLARS	
MEMO Valued employee		Fazbear Entertainment	
⑆ 000045678000 0000⑈ ⑈0000			

THE END

Don't worry, beating Night 5 does not mean it's the end of the game.

EASTER EGG ALERT: 6 A.M. GLITCH

While escaping the wrath of Freddy during a power outage is extremely tough, it isn't impossible. Some players speculate that by playing dead and not moving your cursor, you'll be able to survive until the next night. This isn't confirmed to be true, however. Your best chance of surviving is when it's close to 6 a.m., which is the end of your shift. Sometimes Freddy will not be able to attack because you have reached the end of the night just as you ran out of power and he began his approach.

GAMEPLAY TIP: You can hold C, D, and Num + on your keyboard to skip any night on the PC version of *Five Nights at Freddy's*.

CAM
1B

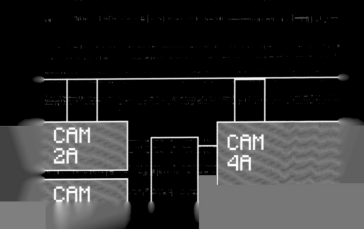

CAM
1C

CAM
2A

CAM
4A

CAM

The animatronics get new designs in *Five Nights at Freddy's 2*.

Five Nights at Freddy's 2 was released on November 11, 2014, after the huge success of the first game. This sequel is hailed as one of the best games in the series by devout *Five Nights at Freddy's* fans. Others criticized this game, however, because of how difficult it is compared to the first game.

The goal of *Five Nights at Freddy's 2* is very similar to its predecessor. As a night guard, it is your job to make sure the roaming animatronics at Freddy Fazbear's Pizza chain do not attack you. Despite the similarities to the first game, you assume the role of a new security guard, Jeremy Fitzgerald, at a different Freddy Fazbear's Pizza location.

FAZBEAR FACT: *FIVE NIGHTS AT FREDDY'S 2* WAS TEASED BY SCOTT CAWTHON ONLY ONE MONTH AFTER THE ORIGINAL *FIVE NIGHTS AT FREDDY'S* WAS RELEASED.

When the game starts, the information about this specific pizzeria location is relayed to you by the man on the phone, still affectionately nicknamed Phone Guy. As the nights progress, you'll learn more and more information from him about the rumor of an ongoing police investigation at the restaurant.

In *FNaF 2*, you play in an entirely different pizzeria than in the first game.

Unlike the original *Five Nights at Freddy's* game, the sequel introduces pixelated mini games that divulge the game's lore. You'll learn about the suspicious events that happened at the pizzeria prior to your shifts there. By the end of the game, you'll eventually learn that multiple children were killed at the restaurant by an unknown person.

FAZBEAR FACT: THOUGH NEVER OFFICIALLY CONFIRMED, PEOPLE SPECULATE THAT PHONE GUY IS THE SAME MAN FROM THE FIRST GAME BECAUSE HIS CHARACTER IS ONCE AGAIN VOICED BY SCOTT CAWTHON.

This game introduces mini games that further explain the game's lore.

Unlike in the original *Five Nights at Freddy's* game, there are no doors leading to the Office. The buttons controlling door locks and lights are gone. Instead, players must use two new tools to protect themselves from the attacking animatronics. The first is a flashlight. Players can now use a flashlight to see into the dark and illuminate the security monitor, and the flashlight also wards off certain animatronics and keeps them at a safe distance. The other tool is a Freddy Fazbear mask, which you can put on to trick the animatronics.

In addition to new mechanics, *Five Nights at Freddy's 2* introduces several new characters.

» TOY ANIMATRONICS

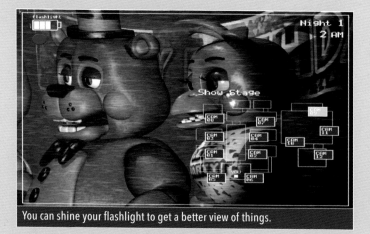

You can shine your flashlight to get a better view of things.

You'll notice the appearance of the same animatronics you've come to know and love: Freddy Fazbear, Chica, Bonnie, and, of course, the ever so lovable Foxy. These animatronics have a different look from the first game, however, as they use different models. They're referred to as toy versions of their original counterparts because these animatronics have a cuter and more bubbly look. While they're less gritty, the new designs don't make them any less scary to players. Some could argue that their innocent appearance is what makes them all the more creepy.

The Toy animatronics have a facial recognition feature and access to a criminal database, which helps them identify harmful people who may want to hurt the children at the restaurant. However, the night mode on these animatronics does not have these added features and instead prompts the characters to gravitate toward the sound of movement, so they may entertain whatever guest is in the area. For the game's purposes, that's *you*, the new night guard.

» WITHERED ANIMATRONICS

Similar to the first game, Withered Freddy can also be seen in this game by the women's bathroom.

In the Parts and Service Area of the restaurant there are broken and partially dismantled versions of Chica, Bonnie, Freddy, and Foxy. They are referred to as Withered animatronics, because they are decrepit and wrecked versions of the animatronics we were introduced to in the first *Five Nights at Freddy's* game. Phone Guy tells us that the Withered animatronics are outdated and only used for spare parts currently. At night, they will roam the pizzeria and try to attack the security guard.

» BALLOON BOY

Balloon Boy is a brand-new animatronic that resembles a young boy. You can find him in the Game Area, acting as a balloon vendor. He wears a red and blue striped button-down shirt, a matching pinwheel hat, and holds a sign that reads "Balloons!" He can leave his spot throughout the night and attack you in the Office by traveling through the vents.

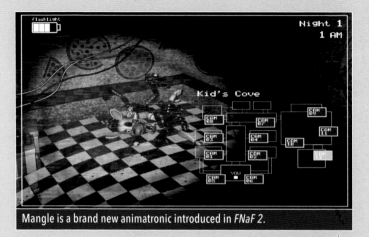

Mangle is a brand new animatronic introduced in *FNaF 2*.

Mangle is the toy version of Foxy. The creators believed that the original Foxy was too scary. Mangle was given white skin, red blushing cheeks, and pink ears to appeal more to children. In Kid's Cove, Mangle is often torn apart and put back together by the kids. Therefore, Mangle is turned into a building attraction where kids can dismantle the animatronic and put it back together. Because of that, his design is the most damaged version of Foxy that players will be introduced to.

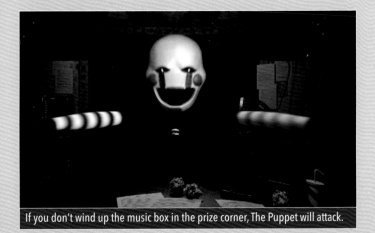

If you don't wind up the music box in the prize corner, The Puppet will attack.

The Puppet has a white face with red blush on its cheeks and purple stripes coming down from its hollowed eyes. The Puppet is long and slender, wearing a black and white striped suit and marionette strings.

If you do not wind up the music box every so often, The Puppet will jump from its hiding spot behind the prize counter and make a move to attack you in the Office.

FAZBEAR FACT: IT IS REVEALED IN THE *TAKE CAKE TO THE CHILDREN* MINI GAME THAT THE PUPPET IS ACTUALLY A CHILD WHO POSSESSED THE ANIMATRONIC AFTER WILLIAM AFTON KILLED HER. (SEE MORE ABOUT WILLIAM AFTON ON PAGE 94.) IN THE *GIVE GIFTS GIVE LIFE* MINI GAME, THE PUPPET PUTS THE SOULS OF THE KIDS FROM THE "MISSING CHILDREN INCIDENT" INTO ANIMATRONICS.

» NEW ROOMS

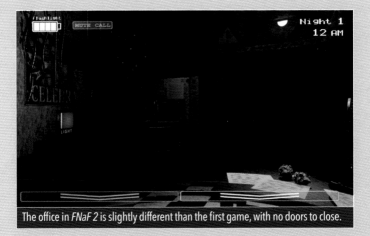

The office in *FNaF 2* is slightly different than the first game, with no doors to close.

Five Nights at Freddy's 2 uses the security monitor in the same way as the first game does. The locations you can look at are slightly different, however. In the sequel, you're able to view Party Rooms 1 to 4, the left and right air vent, the Main Hall, the Show Stage, Parts and Service, Game Area, Prize Corner, and Kid's Cove.

Bonnie remains one of the more aggressive animatronics, despite having a much less sinister look.

Party Room 1 is a small room with a few tables and party hats. You can see it on CAM 01. There is a poster on the wall with toy versions of the animatronics on it. This room is connected to the left air vent. You can see Withered Bonnie, Toy Chica, and Mangle occasionally in this room.

Party Room 2 is discernable by the wet floor sign.

Party Room 2 can be seen on CAM 02. It has a banner with "LET'S PARTY!!!" on it. There's a wet floor sign next to an unidentified liquid.

The tables have red and white stripes on them. This room connects to the right vent. Withered Chica, Toy Bonnie, and Mangle pass through this room. Party Room 3 has the same party tables and decorations as the other rooms. It also has a strange dark substance smeared on the wall and floors. It is located on the left side of the pizzeria. The third party room is one of the least visited locations by the animatronics. However, Toy Bonnie and Withered Freddie can pass through here. Party Room 4 is found on CAM 04. It has a single table with gifts and balloons on it. There are handcrafted paper plate pictures of Bonnie, Freddy, and an unknown character on the wall. There are drawings on the wall that can be seen in other rooms as well. Toy Bonnie, Toy Chica, and Withered Chica can pass through this room.

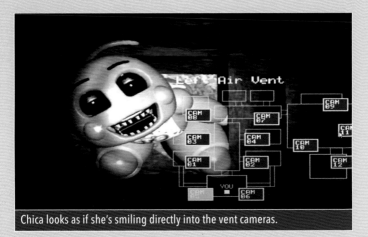

Chica looks as if she's smiling directly into the vent cameras.

There are two vents in *Five Nights at Freddy's 2* that the animatronics use to sneak into the Office. If an animatronic goes through the vent, they'll end up in the vent's blind spot, which can't be seen on the security camera. If this happens, you will only have a few seconds to put on the Freddy Fazbear mask before you are attacked. In order to catch sight of an animatronic in the vent you'll need to use your light. The left vent is used by Toy Chica, Balloon Boy, and Withered Bonnie. The right air vent is used by Mangle, Toy Bonnie, and Withered Chica.

FAZBEAR FACT: IT IS RARE, BUT SOMETIMES YOU MAY CATCH A GLIMPSE OF ENDOSKELETONS CRAWLING THROUGH THE VENTS.

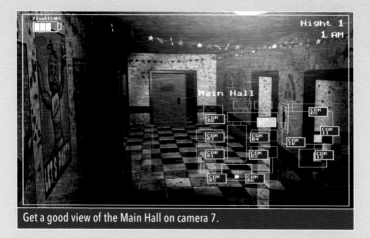

Get a good view of the Main Hall on camera 7.

The Main Hall is connected to the Parts and Service Area as well as the Game Room. It features the familiar black and white checkered flooring and posters of the new toy versions of each animatronic on the walls. You can see the doors to the bathrooms from this security camera. Players will be able to see Toy Chica, Withered Bonnie, Withered Freddy, Mangle, and sometimes The Puppet in the form of a hallucination.

The night will always start with Bonnie, Freddy, and Chica on the show stage.

Similar to the first *Five Nights at Freddy's,* the animatronics will start on the Show Stage every night before leaving to roam the pizzeria. Except, in *Five Nights at Freddy's 2,* it is the toy versions of the animatronics that you will see here. Besides Toy Bonnie, Toy Chica, and Toy Freddy, none of the other animatronics are sighted here. Aside from the animatronics on stage, all you can really make out in this room is the "Happy Birthday" banner on the wall. Toy Freddie cannot leave this area until the other two animatronics leave first.

GAMEPLAY TIP: If all the animatronics leave the Show Stage, you will not be able to use their light in this room.

The Parts and Service Area is where all of the withered animatronics can be found.

Phone Guy tells the player that the animatronics in the Parts and Service Area are older models from a previous pizzeria location that are used for parts. This is where the Withered versions of the animatronics can be found. It is said that this is where Withered Golden Freddy starts as well, but he does not appear on screen like the other animatronics. The first animatronic to leave the Parts and Service Area is Withered Bonnie, followed by Withered Chica, and then lastly Withered Freddy. The Parts and Service Area is extremely dark and you must use your flashlight to view it clearly. The room is dirty and dusty with wires along the wall. There is a mysterious dark substance on the floor.

GAMEPLAY TIP: If every other animatronic has left the Parts and Service Area already, when Withered Foxy is stunned, he will return to this room. So, despite him not showing up on camera in this room at the start of the night, it's possible that he begins in this room and cannot be seen on the security monitor.

EASTER EGG ALERT: SHADOW FREDDY

Shadow Freddy can be encountered in the Parts and Service Area, but it is a rare occurrence. He will be sitting down in the same spot as you will usually see Withered Bonnie. Shadow Freddy resembles Golden Freddy except his coloring is dark purple. If you look at Shadow Freddy for too long, he will crash your game. If you're playing the mobile version, this encounter will freeze your game.

» GAME AREA

Balloon Boy is a new animatronic that is introduced in *Five Nights at Freddy's 2*.

The Game Area is the spawn location for Balloon Boy, a new animatronic introduced in *Five Nights at Freddy's 2*. The only other animatronics who are ever seen in this room are Toy Freddy and Mangle. In the Game Area, there is a carousel with Freddy, Bonnie, Foxy, and Chica-themed characters. On the wall is a "Happy Birthday" banner and on the right there are gift boxes with balloons.

FAZBEAR FACT: THIS IS THE ONLY ROOM ASIDE FROM THE PRIZE CORNER THAT YOU CAN HEAR THE MUSIC BOX PLAYING IN.

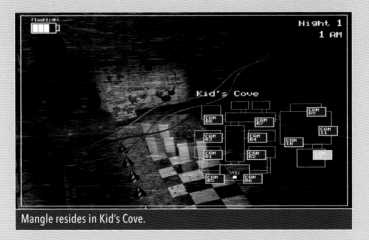

Mangle resides in Kid's Cove.

Kid's Cove is a parallel to Pirate Cove from *Five Nights at Freddy's*. However, the design is more similar to the Party Rooms with gifts on the floor and a table that has party hats on it. The wall has children's drawings with the words "The New Face of Playtime." This is where Mangle will start the night. You'll find him lying on the ground, broken and torn apart. Mangle is the only animatronic you will encounter in this room.

GAMEPLAY TIP: When Mangle leaves Kid's Cove, wires will appear on the walls. Also, when Mangle is in Kid's Cove, an eyeball appears. It disappears when he leaves.

Plushies of the animatronics can be seen in the prize corner.

The Prize Corner can be viewed using CAM 11 on the security monitor and is located on the far right of the restaurant. When you click the video feed, you'll see the pizzeria's classic black and white checkered flooring. You'll also notice plush versions of Freddy, Bonnie, and Chica. There's also a poster on the wall that depicts the updated versions of the three band members and a new face, a white and pink fox named Mangle.

On day 1, the man on the phone tells you that every so often you should go to the Prize Corner and wind up the music box. This will keep The Puppet, a never before seen animatronic, at bay.

FAZBEAR FACT: THERE IS NO VISIBLE MUSIC BOX IN CAM 11'S FEED DESPITE BEING ABLE TO WIND ONE UP IN THIS ROOM.

```
                12:00 AM
                1st Night
```

Night 1 is the easiest of all the nights, so use this time to familiarize yourself with the game's altered mechanics.

Five Nights at Freddy's 2 is much harder than the original game. There are no doors, so you must use a flashlight, a security monitor, and a Freddy Fazbear mask instead. While the flashlight has battery life, you do not need to worry about expending power when using the security monitor or the vents' lights. Each hour of the night lasts one minute and eight seconds. With this information in mind, you'll be able to effectively plan your night.

The Toy animatronics will become active at 2 a.m. You will need to keep an eye on the left and right vents where the animatronics will travel through to get to the Office. You will hear banging sounds to alert you that an animatronic is in one of the vents. To ward off any animatronics you see in the vent, place the Freddy Fazbear mask over your head. You will know they've left the vents once you hear thumping sounds.

Unlike in the first *Five Nights at Freddy's* game, Toy Freddy will be able to move around on the first night. If you notice him peeking into the Office, even closer than he usually does, you'll want to put on the Freddy Fazbear mask.

On this night, you won't have to worry about Withered Foxy attacking. Though some players have reported encountering Foxy, it is highly unlikely. However, it wouldn't be a bad idea to use the flashlight every few moments to check the halls near the Office and make sure no animatronic has gotten too close. Keep in mind, the flashlight has a battery life, so using it too frequently will deplete its power. Be sure to have some battery life left because when Foxy appears in the hall, you'll need to flash your light a few times to keep him away. You can flash your lights on the Show Stage to keep the animatronics frozen there.

Bonnie enjoys taunting players by looking directly into the security cameras.

GAMEPLAY TIP: Flashing your lights on the Show Stage will not keep the animatronics frozen on the Show Stage for the whole night, but it should work until around 4 a.m.

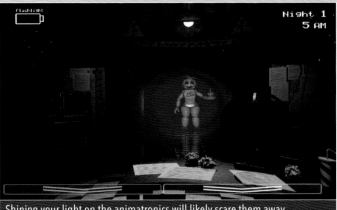

Shining your light on the animatronics will likely scare them away.

The music box in the Prize Corner will remain wound up until 2 a.m. on this night and will begin to wind down after that. Failing to wind the music box up when the music stops will trigger an attack from The Puppet. Players will know that the music is going to stop soon by an orange indicator flashing on their screen. If that notification turns red, it means the song has ended. You will have only a few seconds to wind up the music box if this happens.

There are two recommended strategies for surviving the first night. In the first one, you'll want to check the security monitor and then wind up the music box. After that, you'll lower the monitor and put on the Freddy Fazbear mask to keep away enemies. You'll also want to use your flashlight every so often to check the halls for Foxy.

The second strategy is an easier one that some players may find risky. It requires you to only activate the music box and touch nothing else. This should work because Foxy and the other old animatronics will not be active. Toy Freddy will only attack if you pull down the monitor multiple times, so you'll still be able to check the monitor sparingly if you need to.

FAZBEAR FACT: COMPLETING A SINGLE NIGHT WILL TAKE YOU SIX MINUTES AND FORTY-EIGHT SECONDS.

12:00 AM
2nd Night

Be prepared. Night 2 is slightly more difficult than Night 1.

Similar to the previous game, as nights progress the game gets more difficult. Toy Freddie, Bonnie, and Chica will become more active. Mangle can also leave Kid's Cove as early as midnight. On Night 2, Balloon Boy is activated, adding another animatronic to the nightly list of offenders.

The music box will wind down more quickly on Night 2. So, a good strategy would be to only use the security monitor to check the Prize Corner. This makes it easier and quicker for you to wind the music box when necessary. You'll want to first check the Main Hall on CAM 07, then check the left air vent light. Afterward, check the Main Hall again and then look at the right air vent. Lastly, you'll want to pull up the monitor again and wind up the music box. Don't forget to flash the lights in the Office to check for Foxy. If you see an animatronic in the vent, be sure to place the Freddy Fazbear mask on.

Unfortunately, some animatronics, including Toy Freddie, will stay near the Office entrance for long periods of time. Therefore, you'll need to find a balance between using the Freddy mask and taking it off to wind up the music box and check the vents.

GAMEPLAY TIP: Listen closely for the banging noise of the vents to save you some time checking the monitor!

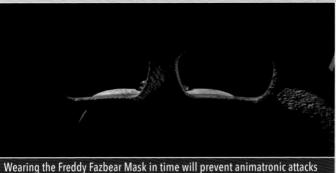

Wearing the Freddy Fazbear Mask in time will prevent animatronic attacks from Bonnie and Chica if they manage to sneak into the office.

On Night 3, the Withered animatronics will become active. This adds another layer of difficulty as you now have to ward off the four new Toy animatronics, four Withered animatronics, Balloon Boy, and The Puppet. However, the Toy animatronics will become slightly less aggressive on this night. Also, the music box continues to wind down faster each and every night.

If Bonnie or Chica manage to enter the Office, you only have a second to put on the Freddy Fazbear mask before being attacked. Bonnie may sometimes disappear after going through the Main Hall to trick you into thinking he has left. In this situation, Bonnie has traveled to Party Room 1, which is only a single room away from the left air vent that Bonnie can use to travel to the Office. You'll want to check the left vent on the monitor and use the vent light. If you don't see Bonnie there, put on your Freddy Fazbear mask immediately.

There are two recommended strategies for completing this night. First, you'll want to check the Main Hall and flash your lights if you see Foxy. Afterward, you'll check both vent lights and flash the hall lights. At this time, you should go and wind up the music box. If you see an animatronic in the Office when you pull down the monitor, put on the Freddy Fazbear mask. Now you'll need to check the air vents again and use the mask if you see an animatronic. Keep doing this until the night ends.

The other strategy is to look only at the Prize Corner on your monitor. You'll want a quick and easy way to wind up the music box and ward off The Puppet. When you lower the monitor, quickly put on the Freddy Fazbear mask. If you don't see any animatronics in the Office, check the halls and the vents. Be sure to flash the lights if you see Foxy. Wind up the music box again and put on the Freddy Fazbear mask. Repeat until the night ends.

Beware of Toy Freddy who will deliver a frightening jumpscare!

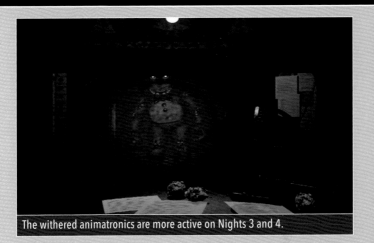

The withered animatronics are more active on Nights 3 and 4.

Similar to Night 3, the Toy animatronics are less active but the Withered versions take on more aggressive roles. From this night on, it becomes increasingly difficult to manage the music box, air vent lights, flashlight, and monitor. Foxy, Balloon Boy, and Mangle are extremely active on this night. Foxy can move as early as 12 a.m. Therefore, you'll need to flash the hall in front of the Office several times throughout the night to catch any nearby animatronics. It is recommended to only watch the Prize Corner on your security monitor.

GAMEPLAY TIP: Be careful because some animatronics will yank down your monitor as you're viewing it. If this happens, you have only a few seconds to put on the Freddy Fazbear mask.

Wind up the music box at the start of the night until either you hear Balloon Boy twice or hear an ambience noise cue play. Then, flash the hallway to scare away any roaming animatronics. Afterward, check the vent lights and put on the Freddy Fazbear mask if you see any hostile animatronics.

Mangle will deliver a terrifying jumpscare if you're not careful.

Night 5 is one of the hardest nights in *Five Nights at Freddy's 2*. Aside from Golden Freddy, all of the animatronics are extremely active. On this night you'll need to have quick reflexes to combat the animatronics.

The recommended strategy is to wait until you hear that one of the animatronics is in the hallway leading to the Office. Wait a total of five seconds before flashing your light toward it. Which animatronic is in the hallway doesn't matter. Once the animatronic is stunned, you'll wind the music box to halfway or three-fourths of the way. If by now you've heard another animatronic, check the hall again and flash your light. If you hear any sounds coming from the vents, be sure to check them. If you see an animatronic, put on the Freddy Fazbear mask. When the animatronic leaves, repeat this process until the end of the night.

Once you beat the night, you'll receive a check made out to Jeremy Fitzgerald for a total of $100.50. The check is dated 1987, years before what takes place in the original *Five Nights at Freddy's*, confirming that *Five Nights at Freddy's 2* is a prequel to the first game. When you return to the main menu, a star will have been granted and you'll be able to access the sixth bonus night.

All animatronics are highly active on the sixth night.

This bonus night is incredibly difficult. All of the animatronics are extremely active, including Golden Freddy. Each animatronic is likely to visit the Office a few times. The music box will also wind down extremely fast. Managing this night will be your greatest challenge yet.

You can use a strategy similar to that in Night 5, but be aware that Golden Freddy is now also a threat. If you notice his head in the back of the hallway when you shine your flashlight, turn it off and wind up the music box. If you see Golden Freddy's entire body in the Office when you pull down the monitor, put on the Freddy Fazbear mask to scare him away.

GAMEPLAY TIP: Make sure the music box ticks at least four to six times when you wind it up.

You will want to use audio cues to help you get through the night. Listening for footsteps to locate which area the animatronics are in will be helpful in saving you time when pulling up the security monitor. You may be able to eliminate using the monitor in some instances. If the sound of footsteps is heavy, as if on metal, there is an animatronic in the air vent.

Another strategy you can use is to shine the flashlight two to four times at the start of the night and wind up the music box for four to six ticks before Phone Guy calls. From here, every single time you lower the monitor, you will want to put on your Freddy Fazbear mask. Then repeat.

Reaching 6 a.m. on this night will earn you a star on the main menu and unlock the custom night.

GAMEPLAY TIP: Every three times you put on the Freddy Fazbear mask, you'll want to check the left air vent light. This eliminates the need to check the right air vent, which will allow more time to dedicate to the music box.

There is a certain level of luck attributed to beating Night 6, as Balloon Boy can sometimes appear in the left vent and will not leave. In this case, if you cannot scare him away before the music box winds down, you will trigger Balloon Boy or The Puppet to attack. You also have to be on the lookout for Foxy.

If you complete Night 6, you'll get another star on the main menu. You'll also receive an overtime check of $20.10.

FAZBEAR FACT: AT THE END OF THIS NIGHT, THERE IS A NEWSPAPER ARTICLE TELLING THE PLAYER THAT THE RESTAURANT IS GOING TO BE CLOSING DOWN AND THE OLDER ANIMATRONICS WILL BE SAVED IN HOPES OF USING THEM AGAIN. THIS IS A NOD TO THE FIRST GAME, WHICH HAS THE OLDER ANIMATRONICS IN PLACE INSTEAD OF THE TOY ANIMATRONICS.

Freddy	Bonnie	Chica	Foxy	BB
< 20 >	< 20 >	< 20 >	< 20 >	< 0 >

Toy Freddy	Toy Bonnie	Toy Chica	Mangle	Golden Freddy
< 0 >	< 0 >	< 0 >	< 0 >	< 0 >

(0-2)easy   (3-6)med   (7-12)hard   (13-20)extreme

There are several in-game unlockables to achieve during the custom night.

Upon completing Night 6, players will unlock the final night, which is the custom night. You will be playing as a new security guard, Fritz Smith, who is promptly fired after completing a custom night successfully. This night allows players to set the AI levels to that of their own choosing. You can tamper with any of the animatronics levels except for The Puppet, whose actions depend on your actions with regard to the music box.

There are several preset levels you can beat that will award you collectibles for the desk in the Office:

20/20/20/20: Set the Withered animatronics to AI level twenty in order to earn a star.

NEW AND SHINY: Set Balloon Boy's, Toy Freddy, Toy Bonnie, Toy Chica, and Mangle's AI levels to ten in order to get a statue of Bonnie playing his guitar.

DOUBLE TROUBLE: Set Withered Bonnie and Toy Bonnie to AI level twenty and Withered Foxy to level five in order to earn a Bonnie Plushie.

NIGHT OF MISFITS: Set Balloon Boy and Mangle up to level twenty and set Golden Freddy to AI level ten in order to get a Balloon Boy statue.

FOXY FOXY: Set Mangle and Withered Foxy to level twenty to get a Foxy Plushie.

LADIES' NIGHT: Set Withered Chica, Toy Chica, and Mangle to level twenty in order to earn a Chica Plushie.

FREDDY'S CIRCUS: Set Withered Freddy and Toy Freddy to level twenty. Set Balloon Boy, Withered Foxy, and Golden Freddy to level ten in order to receive a Freddy Fazbear Plushie.

CUPCAKE CHALLENGE: Set everyone's level to five in order to earn a cupcake Plushie.

FAZBEAR FEVER: Set everyone's levels to ten in order to get Freddy's microphone.

GOLDEN FREDDY: Set everyone's levels to twenty in order to earn a Golden Freddy Plushie.

FAZBEAR FACT: THERE ARE A TOTAL OF 352,716 AI COMBINATIONS YOU CAN HAVE.

By completing certain custom night levels, you can unlock plushies for your desk.

» Play with your volume on. Avoid using the cameras if you don't need to.

» Don't forget to use your Freddy mask.

» You don't need to flash Foxy until he disappears. Then, do it quickly five times in a row.

» Keep an eye on the music box.

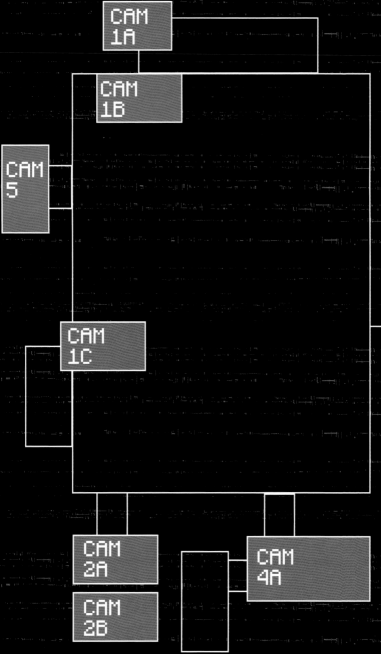

This installment is the first to venture away from the classic pizzeria setting.

Five Nights at Freddy's 3 is the direct sequel to *Five Nights at Freddy's*. It takes place three decades after the original. Unlike the other two games, *Five Nights at Freddy's 3* does not take place in a pizzeria. It takes place in Fazbear's Fright: The Horror Attraction, an attempt at creating an authentic amusement experience of the traumatizing events that happened at the original Freddy Fazbear's Pizza.

This version of the game is slightly different because it doesn't take place in a pizzeria. The Office has a doorway that cannot close or lock. Instead of using a flashlight, locking doors, or wearing a Freddy Fazbear mask, players are forced to rely on their new and improved security monitor system to ward off Springtrap's advances. (See more about Springtrap on page 94.)

FAZBEAR FACT: THE PROTAGONIST OF THIS GAME HAS NO OFFICIAL NAME.

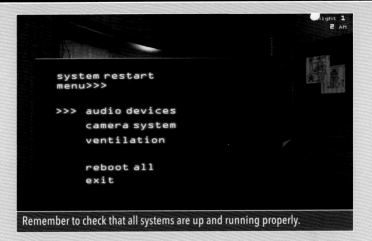

system restart
menu>>>

>>>   audio devices
      camera system
      ventilation

      reboot all
      exit

Remember to check that all systems are up and running properly.

Players have the option to use three different aspects of the security monitor: audio, visuals, and vents. Audio monitoring allows you to play childlike sound effects that lure Springtrap away from the Office. Visual monitoring controls the cameras and can shut off with overuse. Lastly, vent monitoring allows you to seal vents so that Springtrap cannot crawl to you.

FAZBEAR FACT: THIS IS ONE OF THE ONLY GAMES IN THE SERIES THAT DOES NOT FEATURE A VERSION OF FREDDY FAZBEAR IN ITS ICON.

» SPRINGTRAP

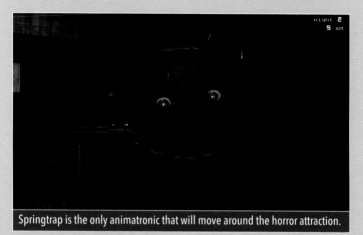

night 2
5 AM

Springtrap is the only animatronic that will move around the horror attraction.

There is only one physical animatronic that can attack you in *Five Nights at Freddy's 3*. He goes by the name of Springtrap. Springtrap used to be a yellow Spring Bonnie animatronic, now tattered and in disrepair like the Withered animatronics in *Five Nights at Freddy's 2*. Springtrap is both an animatronic and a springlock suit that people are able to wear.

By completing each night, similar to *Five Nights at Freddy's 2*, you'll be able to play mini games that will explain some of the game's lore. For example, you'll notice when you look at Springtrap that there are human parts wrapped around the inside of its suit, and you'll discover that it is indeed the corpse of William Afton.

WARNING: This section contains spoilers for the game's ending.

» WHO IS WILLIAM AFTON?

It was confirmed in earlier games that there are souls of children trapped inside the original animatronics from the first game. William Afton is responsible for the murder of the children who found themselves trapped in the animatronics. By playing through the mini games in *Five Nights at Freddy's 3*, you'll find out that William Afton returns to the pizzeria to eliminate the souls of the deceased children. Once the souls are freed, they try to attack William Afton. He runs to the Spring Bonnie suit in an attempt to save himself, but it gets wet and the springlock kills him. This is the version of Springtrap that we see in *Five Nights at Freddy's 3*.

The only other entities in this sequel appear in the form of Phantoms. There are Phantom versions of Freddy, Chica, Foxy, Mangle, The Puppet, and Balloon Boy. While they cannot physically kill you, they allow for openings, like disabling the security cameras, that Springtrap can use to sneak into the Office. They will also deliver a jolting jumpscare.

» WHAT ARE PHANTOMS?

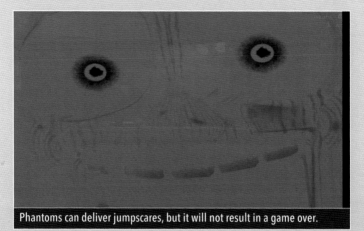

Phantoms can deliver jumpscares, but it will not result in a game over.

Phantom Freddy will reside outside of the Office in the hallway. Phantom Chica will appear on CAM 07. Phantom Balloon Boy can show up on any of the security cameras. Phantom Foxy will appear in the Office. Phantom Mangle will show up on CAM 04 and Phantom Puppet will appear on CAM 08.

» THE OFFICE

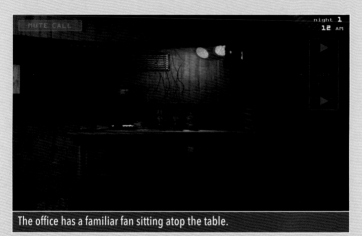

The office has a familiar fan sitting atop the table.

The Office is the player's starting location. You'll see a box of recognizable animatronic parts in the left-hand corner, including Bonnie's signature guitar. There's a front glass where you'll sometimes see Phantom Freddy. On the right-hand side of the screen is your security monitor that will keep track of the ten hallways and additional vent systems. The left side of the Office has an open doorway that leads to a hallway. You can sometimes see Springtrap running across this area or poking his head into the room. You'll also be able to access your maintenance panel from this side of the room. The maintenance panel allows you to reboot any of the monitor systems that may have gone offline during the night.

You can block off vents to prevent Springtrap from entering the office.

There are five vent cameras accessible on the security monitor. Springtrap can travel through all of them. You have the ability to seal these vents, which will prevent Springtrap from entering the Office. Visually, the vents look similar to the ones from *Five Nights at Freddy's 2*.

CAM 11's vent will lead Springtrap to either Hall 7 or Hall 1 if it's not sealed. It features the longest camera angle. CAM 12 will also lead to Hall 1. If Springtrap gets through this vent, he'll most likely be heading to the Office next. CAM 13's is the shortest vent, which connects Hall 1 and Hall 5. CAM 14's vent will lead directly to the Office if it is not sealed off. CAM 15 will connect to Hall 2 and the Office.

GAMEPLAY TIP: CAM 15's vent is likely where a jumpscare will happen if you don't seal it off when Springtrap is there.

You can check for Springtrap in Hall 1.

Halls 1–3 encompass CAM 01, CAM 02, and CAM 03. Hall 1 is characterized by the large exit sign above the doorway. It is the closest to the Office and sits at the left of the map. Not much can be made out because of the angle of the camera, but if Springtrap is in the room you can see him looking directly at the camera. This is the only room in the game where the animatronic has only one position.

FAZBEAR FACT: THE THIRD GAME IN THE FRANCHISE IS THE ONLY ONE TO HAVE DISTINGUISHABLE EXITS. THERE IS ONE IN HALL 1 AND ONE IN HALL 10.

Despite there being a Bonnie suit in Hall 2, Bonnie is not an antagonist in this game.

Hall 2 can be identified by the Hollowed Bonnie suit at the end of the hallway. There are also posters of Freddy, Bonnie, and Chica on the wall. There are four doorways in the room leading to Halls 3, 4, and 5 and the Office. This is the default camera you will start on any given night. Springtrap can appear behind the Bonnie suit or by the doorway to the right.

EASTER EGG ALERT: POSTER ART

On rare occasions, the poster of Freddy Fazbear in Hall 2 can be replaced with an image of Spring Bonnie that has its right eye missing.

Hall 3 is a small corner with mysterious papers all over the floor. Springtrap can appear here in the left of the room or at the bottom right. If he is not in the room, the wires make the security camera look as if the screen is cracked. When he does appear, the wires in the room will disappear.

Keep an eye on the vents leading to Hall 4.

Hall 4 has a lamp on the wall made from a light bulb and an old Foxy animatronic head. You can see the reflection of some of the decorations on the polished floor. There are drawings of Toy Bonnie and Golden Freddy on the walls. You can also see a vent on the floor. Springtrap can appear here hiding in the right-hand corner or in the doorway. Phantom Mangle can also show up here, dangling from the ceiling. If you exit the monitor when this happens, a jumpscare will be triggered in the Office and the audio system will need to be rebooted.

EASTER EGG ALERT: GOLDEN CUPCAKE

Sometimes the picture of Toy Bonnie on the wall can be replaced with the image of a cupcake. On rare occasions the frosting can be golden.

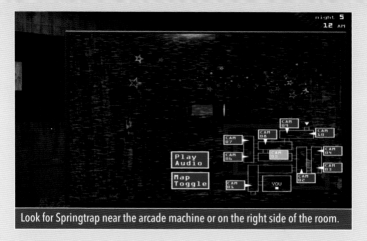

Look for Springtrap near the arcade machine or on the right side of the room.

Hall 5 has an arcade machine that flickers on and off at the far end of the hall. There are glowing white stars that hang from the ceiling. Giant pizza signs hang on the right wall. The left wall has posters of Bonnie and Chica. Hall 5 has the Fazbear Pizza's classic checkered flooring. Springtrap can reveal himself here either by the arcade machine or in the far right of the room.

Hall 6 is shown on CAM 06 with an overhead angle. A bird's-eye view of an arcade cabinet can be seen. There are wires hanging from the ceiling and two doorways. Springtrap can be seen either in the doorway or by the arcade cabinet.

Players can spot Chica's head in the corner of the room.

Hall 7 has two vents, one on the left and one on the right. It has the classic black and white checkered flooring. There is an arcade cabinet in this room with a picture of Freddy Fazbear above it. Springtrap will appear in one of two spots, either the doorway or the far left.

GAMEPLAY TIP: At times an image of Phantom Chica can pop up on the screen of the arcade cabinet in this location. If this happens, when you lower the security monitor, you will get a jumpscare.

EASTER EGG ALERT: MANGLE'S QUEST

Once in Hall 7 on Night 2, if you press the buttons on the top left, bottom left, top right, and then bottom right of the arcade cabinet, you can activate a mini game called *Mangle's Quest*. In *Mangle's Quest*, you have to gather all four of Mangle's body parts to reassemble the animatronic. If you have done the other mini game *BB's Air Adventure* already, you can activate a secret ending for this mini game. You'll also unlock a child wearing a Foxy mask in the *Happiest Day* mini game.

The first thing you'll probably notice in Hall 8 is the Hollowed Chica head on the ground with a light inside of it. There's a vent next to this spot. On the right, you may also notice an image of The Puppet. On the left, there are children's drawings of Balloon Boy, The Puppet, Freddy Fazbear, and Toy Bonnie. Springtrap will appear in the back of the hallway or in the middle.

Complete the secret mini game *BB's Air Adventure* to unlock lore.

EASTER EGG ALERT: BB'S AIR ADVENTURE

By clicking twice on the Balloon Boy poster in Hall 8, you'll be able to play the *BB's Air Adventure* mini game. You take the role of Balloon Boy in this mini game and have to collect balloons. There are a total of eight, but you can reach the ending by grabbing all seven balloons in the first room. However, you can reach a secret room by jumping from the top left corner of the first room. You'll find another exit door that will earn the second ending. In the third ending, as long as you already went through this second exit door, you will be able to jump off a platform to the right. This will reveal the last balloon, which will unlock another ending. Be sure to enter this room from the bottom left corner to avoid having to start from the beginning. To unlock the special cake ending you'll need to have beaten Mangle's Quest first and then return to this mini game. You'll go to the secret room from the last ending, except this time a cake will appear when you approach the child in the room. This will unlock another child in the *Happiest Day* mini game.

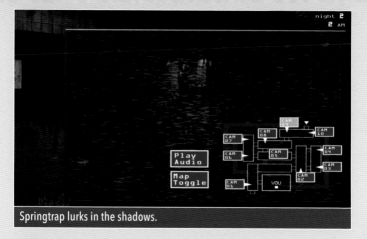

Springtrap lurks in the shadows.

CAM 09 shows a long dark Hall 9 with barely any decorations. There is a vent on the left wall and a poster of Bonnie. You can also see an exit door. You can barely make out what is on the right wall because it is covered in dark shadows. You'll catch sight of Springtrap either in the middle of the hallway or staring directly into the camera on the left side.

Hall 10 is the exit of the Fazbear Fright exhibition. This room is supposed to lead into Hall 1. You can catch sight of the bottom of a red glowing exit sign to the left. There is a cartoon Freddy Fazbear poster on a wall to the right. Sometimes this poster will change to an image of Spring Bonnie. Springtrap will appear in this room with his head staring into the right side of the camera or standing in the corner of the room.

Give out cupcakes in the mini game called *Chica's Party*.

EASTER EGG ALERT: CHICA'S PARTY

On Night 3, four shadow cupcakes will appear on the cameras. You have to click them in a specific order to trigger a special mini game. Find the shadow cupcake in CAM 02, CAM 03, CAM 04, and CAM 06 to start the *Chica's Party* mini game. In this hidden mini game, you play as Chica, who wants to give out cupcakes to crying children. You can earn the first basic ending by giving the four kids cupcakes and walking to the unlocked ending. To unlock the second ending, you'll need to have gotten the cake endings for all the other mini games. Once you have done that and given each crying child their cupcake, you can go to the top left of the bottom level and jump through an invisible hole in the wall. From here you need to land on the red balloon. Doing so will unlock a new child in the *Happiest Day* mini game.

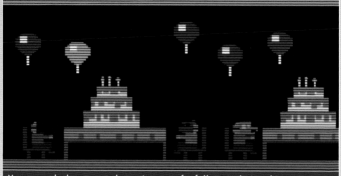

You can unlock a star on the main menu for fully completing this mini game.

EASTER EGG ALERT:
THE HAPPIEST DAY PUPPET MINI GAME

This is the last hidden mini game that you can unlock. You can unlock this mini game on any night by going to CAM 03 and clicking twice on The Puppet drawing on the wall. In this mini game you play as a child wearing a Puppet mask. You can move to the right to find a crying child and several people wearing different animatronic masks. This is dependent on how many of the cake endings you've unlocked in the other five mini games. If you've unlocked them all, a cake will appear on the table if you run into it. Then, the child on the right who is crying will get a Golden Freddy mask. Completing this sequence will unlock a star on the main menu.

The box of animatronics on the floor is a nod to older games.

Night 1 of *Five Nights at Freddy's 3* is impossible to lose. The main goal of this night is to introduce the player to the new mechanics of the game. Springtrap will not be active until the next night. So, use this night to explore the cameras and get a feel for how to use the maintenance panel.

FAZBEAR FACT: THIS IS THE FIRST GAME IN THE FRANCHISE TO HAVE THE FIRST DAY VOID OF ANY ANIMATRONICS ATTACKING.

```
12:00 AM
2ND NIGHT
```

Springtrap will be much more active on the second night.

On Night 2 you will be able to encounter Springtrap and two Phantoms, Mangle and Balloon Boy. You want to use the childlike audio clip of Balloon Boy to lure Springtrap away from your location and into another room. When you first start the night, open the security monitor and locate Springtrap. When you find him, go to a room that is near to him but far away from the Office. Play the audio file there to lure Springtrap away. If you can't find Springtrap on the security cameras, it means he may be in the vents. Switch your security monitor to the vent cams and look for him quickly. Seal the vent pathway he is trying to travel through to block his entry into the Office.

Remember, when you encounter a Phantom, it will force a jumpscare onto you. These jumpscares will not end your game, but they can mess up your audio, cameras, or vent system. Therefore, avoiding them will save you time and having to reboot systems.

GAMEPLAY TIP: Phantom Balloon Boy is active tonight, so if you see him show up on one of the cameras, quickly switch to another one. Do not look at him. You can also run into Phantom Mangle on CAM 04.

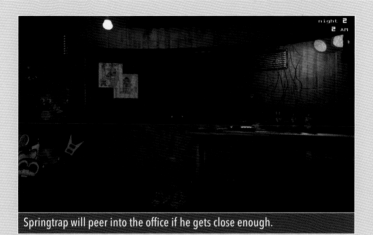

Springtrap will peer into the office if he gets close enough.

Keep in mind that Springtrap will only travel into adjacent rooms. Playing the audio clip in a room that isn't connected to the one Springtrap is in will be useless. You'll want to keep Springtrap in the same few rooms if you can. This way, you can keep a close eye on him and keep him away from the Office.

Try to lure Springtrap to Hall 9 if he isn't there already. Once there, you can switch to the vent cams and seal off the pathway near CAM 11. If Springtrap goes into the vents, play the audio log in Hall 9 again to lure Springtrap back. You can follow this process throughout the night.

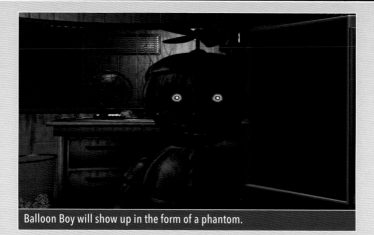
Balloon Boy will show up in the form of a phantom.

On this night, Phantom Foxy, Phantom Chica, and Phantom Freddy are activated. The Phantoms are generally more aggressive, so keep an eye out for them. If you see Phantom Freddy in the Office window, pull up your security monitor or maintenance panel to avoid getting jumpscared.

A good strategy is to locate Springtrap on the cams and pull him away from the Office by using the audio lure. If Springtrap is not on any of the cameras, look for him in the vents and seal whichever one he is in. Then, lure him to another room using an audio lure. Be careful. Using the monitor for too long will cause the cameras to shut down and they'll need to be rebooted.

Don't forget to use an audio lure if you see Springtrap!

If Springtrap pokes his head into the Office, pull up the security monitor and try to lure Springtrap to Hall 1. You can also try and lure Springtrap to Hall 5, reboot your audio system, and then play the audio in Hall 8. This is an attempt to bypass Springtrap having to go through Halls 6 and 7.

You can also play the audio lure in the room that Springtrap was formerly in to keep him in the same area. This will allow you to use the audio lure sparingly and not have to reboot the system as often.

If you see both Phantom Freddy and Springtrap by the Office, pull up your monitor to avoid triggering a Phantom Freddy attack and lure Springtrap to another camera.

GAMEPLAY TIP: If your systems need to be rebooted and it's close to 5 a.m., you can simply look at Springtrap until the night ends.

PRO TIPS

* If you see Springtrap, use an audio lure to move him to another room. Keep in mind that he will only hear the sound from one room away. If he's farther away than that, it will be a waste of a lure.

* Resetting all downed systems, as opposed to resetting them one by one, will save you time.

* If Springtrap moves to a room, seal the vent in that room to prevent him from crawling inside of it.

* Do not leave the vents shut down for too long, as this will cause a sound to play that will lure Springtrap to your office immediately.

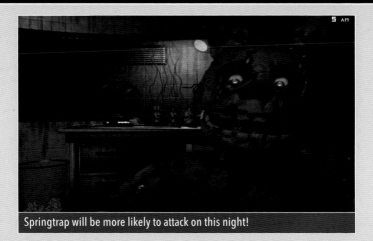

Springtrap will be more likely to attack on this night!

Phantom Puppet becomes active on Night 4. The other Phantoms and Springtrap are more aggressive on this night than on other nights. A good strategy to survive this night is to play an audio lure on CAM 08. You'll reboot anything that may have gone offline, and then double-check the vents to make sure Springtrap hasn't gotten into any of them. If he has, be sure to seal the offending vent shut and lure Springtrap to another room.

The Phantom Puppet usually shows itself on CAM 08, so if you see its face be sure to switch to another camera quickly. If you are not able to, not only will you get a jumpscare, but also your vents and camera will become disabled and you'll need to reboot them as soon as possible.

After rebooting your system, you'll want to check the ventilation system and block off Springtrap if necessary. The rest of the night is pretty straightforward and you can use the tips from previous nights to help you survive this one.

FAZBEAR FACT: IN THE *STAGE01* MINI GAME, "395248" IS THE COLOR CODE FOR PURPLE.

EASTER EGG ALERT: STAGE01

You can unlock Golden Freddy's hidden mini game, called *Stage01*, on this night. In the Office, there are a set of nine clickable wall tiles near the box of animatronic heads. Click the tiles in the order 395248 to access this mini game.

You will play this mini game as Golden Freddy in Freddy Fazbear's Pizza. To achieve the basic ending, all you have to do is walk to the end of the first room and reach the exit door. To achieve the special cake ending, first go to the left near the stage to get to the next room. Then, go to the bottom right of the room and jump in the left portion. Jump left again into the next room, and then up from the middle center of the room. In this room, jump right and then jump up near Spring Bonnie. Jump to the left from this room and you will meet the crying child. As long as you've reached every single other cake mini game ending, you can give the crying child cake and unlock a new kid in the *Happiest Day* mini game.

Unlock Golden Freddy's hidden game on Night 4.

Try to lure Springtrap into Hall 1 with an audio lure if you can.

This is one of the hardest nights of the game. Both Springtrap and the Phantom animatronics are extremely active. You must be quick when checking the security monitor to avoid being jumpscared by one of the Phantoms. If you see Springtrap in a specific room, play the audio lure to keep him in that room. Then, you have time to reboot any systems that may have gone offline. Seal off any vents that Springtrap may enter. If you see him poking his head into the Office doorway, you'll only have a few seconds to play an audio lure in another nearby room to get him to move there instead.

Another strategy is to try and lure Springtrap into Hall 1 with an audio lure. He may move into this room and bypass the Office. This is very risky, but if done correctly it can offer you some safety. You should only exit the monitor when you see Springtrap in this room; otherwise, it means he may be in the Office and ready to attack. If you suspect that Springtrap is hidden behind the monitor in the Office, you may be out of luck. If you pull down the monitor and Springtrap does not attack you, look to your left and avoid making contact until you suspect Springtrap has left the Office. However, this may only work if you are nearing 6 a.m.

Once you complete this night, you will earn your first star on the main menu. You will also get an image of five animatronic heads at the end of this night. If you've reached the bad ending, all five will be lit up to signify that the children's souls are still trapped inside of the animatronics.

Reaching 6 a.m. on Night 5 will end the game.

EASTER EGG ALERT: SHADOW BONNIE

In the Office there is a hard to see area with Plushie animatronics. In the shadow to the right of this is an image of Shadow Bonnie. Click it to activate the last hidden mini game. Continue to press down on the arrow keys to get through the previously played mini games. You'll stop when you run into a child in the bottom left of the screen. You'll need to use a corner glitch that you used in BB's Air Adventure to reach him. When you do reach the kid, you'll give him a piece of cake.

After this is complete, go to CAM 03 and click The Puppet poster to be brought to his mini game. With Shadow Bonnie's mini game complete, you'll be able to give the last remaining child cake, freeing the children's souls and putting them to rest. When you complete the fifth night and this mini game sequence, the ending screen will show five animatronic heads with no lights, signifying the souls of the children have left them.

Shadow Bonnie has his own hidden mini game.

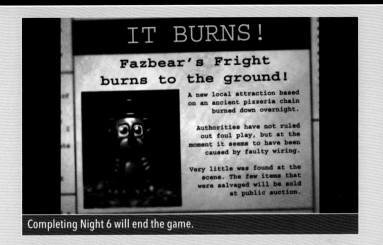

Completing Night 6 will end the game.

Nightmare is the sixth and last playable night in *Five Nights at Freddy's 3*. There is no seventh custom night because the game only has one animatronic. This is the hardest level to beat and in doing so will earn you a second star on their main menu. It will also unlock the jumpscare and cheats tab in the extra menu on the title screen.

A good strategy for completing this night is to avoid rebooting all systems at once. This takes a lot of time. Focus on rebooting each of the audio systems as they go down. This will ensure you have a strategy to lure Springtrap away from the Office while you reboot the other systems. Your next priority should be to reboot the ventilation system so that you're able to seal the vents shut if Springtrap crawls into them.

If Springtrap is looking into the Office, try to use an audio lure to get him into Hall 1 or Hall 2. At 5 a.m., if Springtrap is not around, you can reset the ventilation system and then look to your left to stall him. This will prevent you from having to open the monitor or maintenance panel and trigger a jumpscare.

You can also focus your attention on cameras 09 and 10. If you flick between the two cameras quickly, you'll be able to ward off an attack from Balloon Boy. You'll also be able to tell whether Springtrap has made a move. You can seal the vent in CAM 14, as this one leads directly to the Office. That will buy you some time to lure Springtrap back to Hall 10.

CAM
1A

CAM
1B

CAM
1C

CAM
2A

CAM
4A

CAM

FIVE NIGHTS AT FREDDY'S 4

Five Nights at Freddy's 4 takes place in the crying child's home.

Five Nights at Freddy's 4 was released on July 23, 2015. It's the last game in the main *Five Nights at Freddy's Saga*. Unlike the other games in the series, the game doesn't take place in a pizzeria or an amusement attraction. You don't take the role of security guard at all. Rather, the story takes place in 1983, making it chronologically the first game in the series' lore. You play as a child who needs to keep the scary animatronics out of your bedroom. The only tools you have are a flashlight to ward off the enemy and your ears to listen to any animatronics that may be approaching. You'll also be able to physically move around the room for the first time in a *Five Nights at Freddy's* game.

This game relies heavily on the use of audio to notify the player where an animatronic is so they can flash their light toward it. You will not be able to track movements on a security monitor and you will not receive any encouraging messages from Phone Guy. The gameplay is much slower paced.

In *Five Nights at Freddy's 4*, you are up against Nightmare versions of the animatronics. These are visual entities as opposed to physical animatronics like in the first two games. The game features Nightmare Freddy, Nightmare Bonnie, Nightmare Chica, Nightmare Foxy, and a new animatronic called Plushtrap. The Nightmare animatronics are grotesque versions of the characters players have grown familiar with. They have ten fingers, claws, metallic eyes, and a lot of long, sharp teeth. These animatronics are particularly bloodthirsty.

Nightmare is shrouded in darkness.

» WHO IS NIGHTMARE?

Nightmare is a powerful antagonist in *Five Nights at Freddy's 4*. He looks like Nightmare Freddy except he's shrouded in darkness and his top hat and bow tie are yellow. Underneath the dark shadow, you can see Nightmare's innards. His head resembles the shape of a human skeleton. Nightmare appears at 4 a.m. on the later nights and replaces all of the animatronics and their duties. He is a very aggressive animatronic to combat. Not much else is known about him or how he came to be.

Plushtrap will show up in his own mini game each night.

Five Nights at Freddy's 4 has mini games in between each night, similar to previous installments in the franchise. Plushtrap is the main character of his own mini game, *Fun with Plushtrap*. In this mini game, Plushtrap is sitting on a chair at the end of a really dark hallway. You have to shine your flashlight on him once he hits the X mark on the floor. If you successfully achieve this, you'll earn a two-hour bonus on the night, making it start at 2 a.m. instead of 12 a.m.

FAZBEAR FACT: PLUSHTRAP IS A SMALLER PLUSH VERSION OF SPRINGTRAP FROM *FIVE NIGHTS AT FREDDY'S 3.*

In the special Halloween update, Marionette replaces Nightmare Freddy.

Five Nights at Freddy's 4 received a special Halloween update. It replaced all of the animatronics with different ones. Instead of Nightmare Bonnie and Nightmare Chica, the Halloween Edition swaps in Jack-O-Bonnie and Jack-O-Chica, pumpkin-themed variants of the beloved animatronics. Nightmare Mangle replaces Nightmare Foxy, and Nightmare Balloon Boy replaces Plushtrap. Nightmare is replaced with Nightmarionne, a Nightmare version of The Puppet. There are also Halloween decorations added to the game.

FAZBEAR FACT: THIS GAME WAS ORIGINALLY NAMED *FIVE NIGHTS AT FREDDY'S 4: THE FINAL CHAPTER* DURING DEVELOPMENT UNTIL THE LAST PART WAS DROPPED FROM THE TITLE.

» BEDROOM

You can move around the crying child's bedroom.

The Bedroom encompasses the entire map of *Five Nights at Freddy's 4*. With the exception of mini games, you will be mostly staying inside this room as the nights progress. There are two doors leading to the hallways on either side of the room. Another door on the wall leads to the closet, where you can see a few shirts hanging. There are two dressers in the room with several decorations on top. Lastly, you can find a bed with a Freddy Fazbear Plushie sitting on top.

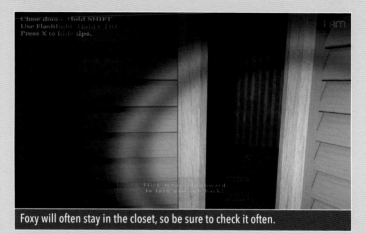

Foxy will often stay in the closet, so be sure to check it often.

The Closet is where Nightmare Foxy resides. If you block him from attacking, he will be replaced with a Foxy Plushie. You can also see Nightmare Freddy in the Closet on the later nights. By design, the Closet isn't anything extravagant. It has white doors that open to the left and right. Some clothing can be seen through the dark crack in the middle of the doors' opening.

GAMEPLAY TIP: While Foxy's head can poke out from the closet, no jumpscares occur in this area.

FAZBEAR FACT: IF YOU FEND OFF NIGHTMARE MANGLE IN THE CLOSET, HE WILL BE REPLACED WITH A PLUSHIE. THIS MAKES MANGLE THE ONLY CHARACTER IN THE SERIES TO RECEIVE A PLUSHIE VARIANT BUT NOT A FIGURINE.

» BED

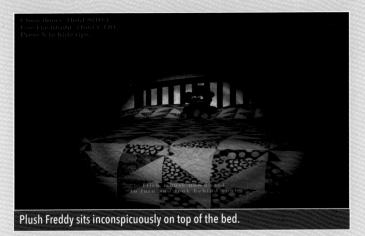

Plush Freddy sits inconspicuously on top of the bed.

This twin-size bed has a white quilt with brown, yellow, and blue designs.
A Freddy Fazbear Plushie sits innocently on top of the bed. From the angle
we approach the bed, the floor cannot be seen. Sometimes on the bed,
three small versions of Nightmare Freddy will appear. These small guys,
known as Freddles, try and summon Nightmare Freddy to attack you.
You can use your flashlight to scare them away, but they become more
aggressive as the nights go on.

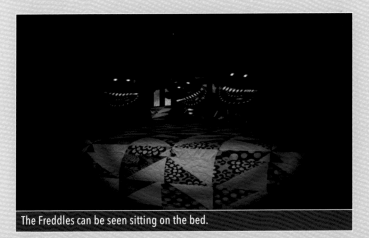

The Freddles can be seen sitting on the bed.

Nightmare Chica and Nightmare Bonnie will use the halls to get to the bedroom.

The Right Hall is long and has red checkered walls, unlike the blue ones in the bedroom. It has two windows and a few pictures on the wall. Nightmare Chica and Nightmare Foxy can be seen traveling through this hallway from the first night. However, Nightmare Foxy will move to the Bedroom before attacking. Nightmare Freddy and Nightmare can make appearances here in later nights.

Look closely and you'll see pictures on the hallway walls.

Similar to the Right Hall, the Left Hall is long and shares the same red checkered wall pattern. There are two lights that the player can see and some pictures on the wall. Instead of Nightmare Chica, Nightmare Bonnie will appear in this hallway and can come as early as Night 1. Nightmare Foxy can also make an appearance, but he will run to the Bedroom before attacking you. Nightmare Freddy and Nightmare can also appear in the Left Hall in later nights.

FAZBEAR FACT: IT IS BELIEVED THAT THE PICTURES ON THE HALLWAY WALLS ARE OF SCOTT CAWTHON AND HIS FAMILY.

This game features title cards that show what night the player is on.

Unlike with the previous games in the *Five Nights at Freddy's Saga*, there is no guy on the phone to tell you how to play. Instead, the tutorial tips will pop up on the screen for you. Similar to *Five Nights at Freddy's 3*, the first day acts mostly as a way for the player to get used to the game's new mechanics. The first Nightmare animatronic will not start moving until about three hours into the night.

GAMEPLAY TIP: Make sure you are wearing headphones and there is no background noise that can be heard. Listening to the animatronics is crucial in this game, as there is no security monitor to tell you where they are at any given time.

There are two things you'll need to do to survive this night. First, you'll want to shine your flashlight on the bed every so often to keep the Freddles at bay. Do not shine it for a prolonged period of time because you can end up summoning Nightmare Foxy instead. Next, you'll want to go to both the Left and the Right Hall doors. You'll want to listen for about four seconds at each. If you hear breathing, it is either Nightmare Chica or Nightmare Bonnie. Shut the door to prevent them from attacking. You'll hear the animatronics walking away once the door is closed.

GAMEPLAY TIP: If when you approach the door, you can't hear any breathing, be sure to shine the flashlight into the hallway to scare away any animatronics that may be approaching.

Close doors- Hold SHIFT
Use Flashlight- Hold CTRL
Press X to hide tips.

! WARNING !

Listen carefully! If you hear
breathing, hold the door shut!

If you do not hear breathing,
then use your flashlight!

Click mouse downward
to turn and run back!

This game will have players relying heavily on visual and audio cues.

BE CAREFUL: If you shine the flashlight in the hall while the animatronic is close enough that you hear its breathing, you will most likely be attacked. If the animatronic is down the hall and you don't shine the light on it, when you open the door the animatronic will run toward you and attack. Bonnie and Chica will work in tandem. If you pay too much attention to one, the other will take advantage and sneak in. Use your time wisely and pay attention to the audio cues.

4 days until the party.

Each night, a mini game featuring the crying child will play out.

Starting on Night 2, all of the animatronics will begin to become more aggressive. You need to actively listen for breathing and footsteps to combat both Nightmare Bonnie and Nightmare Chica. However, be mindful that this night introduces some new sound effects to confuse players.

Like the night before, you'll want to shine your flashlight on the bed to ward off the Freddles. You'll also want to approach the hall doors and listen for breathing. If you hear breathing, shut the door until you hear the animatronic's footsteps leaving. Then, shine your light to keep it at bay. Be sure to check both sides because while one is distracting you, the other might sneak in from the other side to attack.

Foxy will begin to be more active in the Closet on this night. You'll have to dedicate some of your time and attention to this area. Foxy will start as a Plushie but as he gets more threatening he'll evolve into Nightmare Foxy in a position that shows he's ready to pounce out of the Closet. If this happens, you need to hold the Closet doors for long enough that Nightmare Foxy turns back into a Plushie. While the doors are shut, you can go back and check on the Left and Right Hall doors.

GAMEPLAY TIP: Foxy will often attack when the player's back is turned and their attention is on the bed.

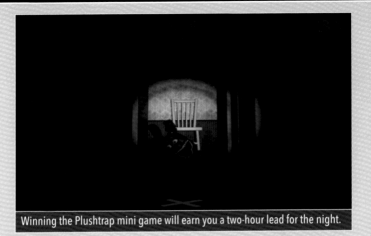

Winning the Plushtrap mini game will earn you a two-hour lead for the night.

If you pass the Plushtrap mini game, you will have two fewer hours to worry about. Try to aim for successful completion of this mini game each night. You'll want to use the same strategy as before, but keep in mind that the animatronics are much more aggressive as the nights go on. Foxy's timer to morph and attack is much shorter, so you have to be mindful to block his attacks while also warding off Nightmare Bonnie, Nightmare Chica, and the Freddles.

If you hear the sound of quick footsteps, almost sprinting, while you're at one of the hall doors, you'll want to check the Closet because this likely means Foxy's transformation timer has begun. Be sure to check often on the Freddles and the hall doors for Bonnie and Chica.

Foxy will deliver a terrifying jumpscare if left unchecked.

On Night 4, you should focus on keeping Foxy out of the Closet. Shining your light on him will prolong his time. If you hear the Freddles screaming, it means they are getting restless and you need to check on the bed. The best course of action is to find a pattern that works for you (such as checking each hall, the closet, and then the bed) and sticking to it.

FAZBEAR FACT: THIS IS THE LAST NIGHT THAT ALL OF THE ANIMATRONICS WILL BE ACTIVE AT ONCE.

Plush Golden Freddy can be seen in a mini game.

On Night 5, only Nightmare Freddy is active. This does not mean that you have any less to worry about, however. Instead of breathing by the doors, you'll hear laughter. When laughter plays alongside footsteps, this means that Nightmare Freddy has broken into the Bedroom and can make his way to the bed or the Closet. If you hear laughter followed by footsteps, then Nightmare Freddy is at one of the hall doors.

Unfortunately, Nightmare Freddy can move from one hall to the next rather quickly, so be sure to listen for any audio clues, especially footsteps, that indicate he has changed spots.

If you see Nightmare Freddy in the hallway, you have to shut the door as quickly as you can. Do not let go of the door until you hear footsteps taking Freddy away from the doorway. If he's on the bed, you'll need to flash your light at him until he leaves.

GAMEPLAY TIP: If you spot Nightmare Freddy in the Closet, you need to shut the door until you hear him go away.

Completing Night 5 will unlock the "Extras" menu and a star on the main menu.

Use the arrow keys to move the child around.

In this series of mini games playable at the end of each night, you'll find more about the game's lore and the infamous Bite of '83 at Freddy Fazbear's Pizza. The first mini game starts with a countdown of five days until a party. You take the role of the crying child who is scared of Freddy Fazbear and the other animatronics because of the actions of his older brother. For most of the nights, it will end with the crying child's older brother jumping out in an animatronic mask to scare the young boy. The young boy will fall to the floor with more visible tears, and "Tomorrow is another day" will appear on the screen.

By the final mini game, you will find out a particularly tragic part of the game's lore. The crying child, at Freddy Fazbear's Pizza in 1983, runs to the door to escape his birthday party. However, he is stopped by his older brother and a few of the boy's friends. They pick up the crying child and bring him to get a closer look at Freddy Fazbear, who ends up biting and killing the young child. We find out later that the murdered child is the youngest son of William Afton, the creator of the animatronics.

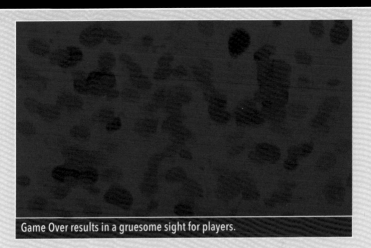
Game Over results in a gruesome sight for players.

This is a bonus night. All of the Nightmare animatronics are extremely active this night. They will stop at nothing to catch you off guard. At around 4 a.m., Nightmare, the more aggressive and frightening counterpart to Nightmare Freddy, will take over the role of all of the animatronics.

As this night is a combination of Night 4 and Night 5, you will want to use strategies from both of those nights. When Nightmare is in the room, the sound of breathing will be gone. In place there will be laughter, similar to Nightmare Freddy. Instead of Freddles showing up on the bed to summon Nightmare Freddy, you will see miniature Nightmare heads on the bed to signify he is coming.

Nightmare Chica appears as one of the most chilling versions of herself.

GAMEPLAY TIP: Don't spend too much time on this night trying to get Foxy down to his Plushie version. If Foxy is in a standing position, you still have time to check both the bed and the hall doors. Listen for breathing and footsteps, and flash the light on the bed if you see the Freddles.

At the end of Night 6, you will watch a final cutscene that ends the events of the mini game. The young boy's brother apologizes to him for what he did. The animatronic toys tell the boy they are still his friend. At the very end we hear someone say, "I will put you back together," but it is unclear who says this or what it means.

When this is complete, you will be brought to the main menu, where you will be given another star.

Nightmare Bonnie's jumpscare is terrifying.

Night 7, known as Nightmare, is unlocked after the completion of Night 6. It can be played from the "Extras" menu on the title screen. *Five Nights at Freddy's 4* brings back the custom night except it offers specific challenge modes you can try to complete. The four challenges you can complete are as follows.

» BLIND MODE

In this mode, the screen is completely black. You have no time indicator on the screen to tell you how far along in the night you are. You have to play through the game until you either complete the night or are jumpscared. As you can imagine, this is pretty difficult to complete, especially if you don't know the game's layout like the back of your hand.

GAMEPLAY TIP: Because you won't be able to see whether Nightmare Foxy has turned back into a Plushie when you're in Blind Mode, you should hold the door closed for six seconds. Listen to audio clues very closely and try to know where you are at all times.

» MAD FREDDY MODE

In this mode, Nightmare Freddy is more active than he has been in the other nights. This does not eliminate the other animatronics, however. At 4 a.m., Nightmare will replace all of the other animatronics. But until then, you want to make sure you are constantly flashing the bed to remove the Freddles. Nightmare Foxy should be kept out of the Closet for as long as possible before shutting the doors to save you time.

» INSTA-FOXY MODE

This game mode plays out normally except Nightmare Foxy is in the Closet at the start of the night. Use the strategies from previous nights to complete this.

» ALL NIGHTMARE MODE

In this mode, Nightmare is the only active animatronic for the entirety of the night. Use the strategies from the other nights, particularly Nights 4 and 5, to help complete this challenge.

Completing Night 7 will earn you a third star on the main menu.

The first time Foxy enters the fourth stage, he'll deliver a jumpscare, but it won't end the game.

» Get a reliable pair of headphones because this game is unplayable without sound.

» If you hear footsteps, close the corresponding door.

» If you hear pots and pans, this means that Chica is in the kitchen and you have some time before she reaches the bedroom.

» There will be a maximum of three Freddles on the bed before they attack.

» Foxy cannot enter the closet if you are looking at the door that he's trying to run to.

» When Foxy finishes his fourth stage, he'll deliver a spooky jumpscare.

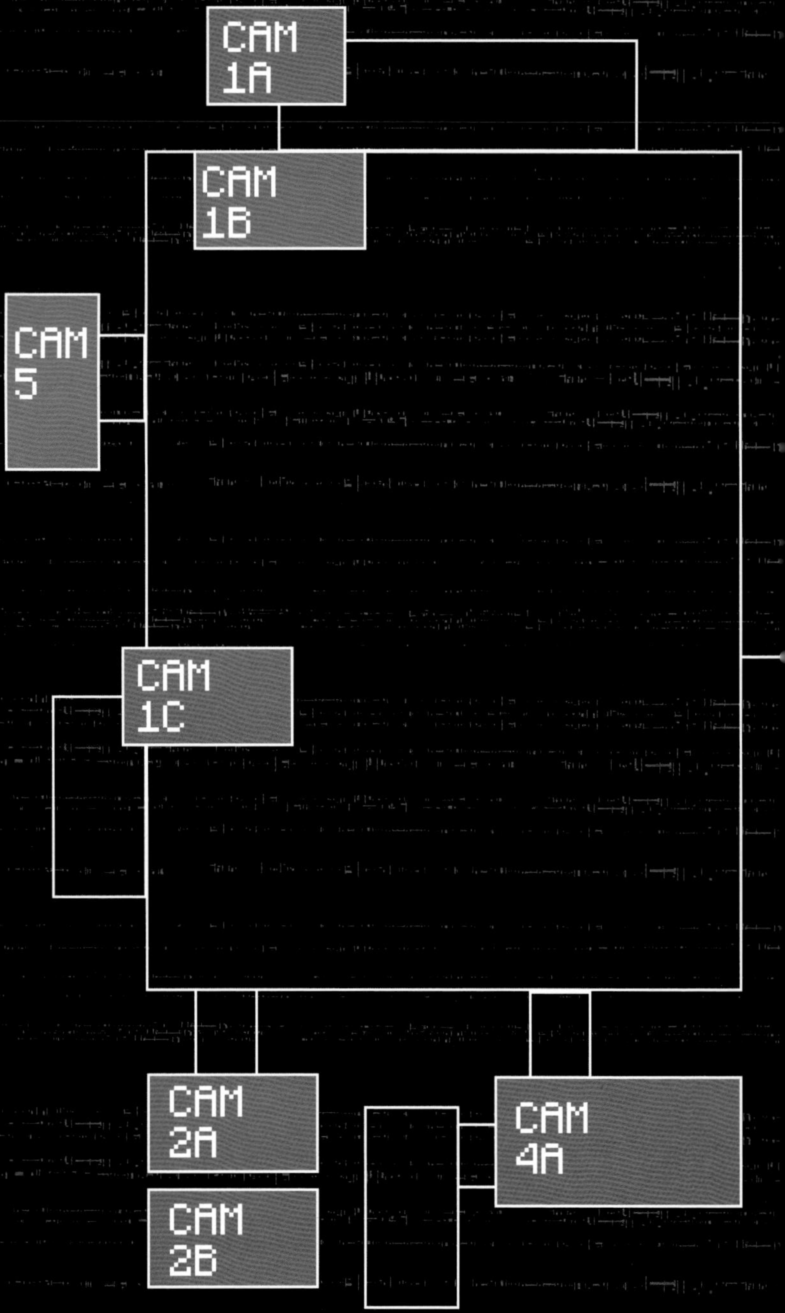
CAM 1A
CAM 1B
CAM 5
CAM 1C
CAM 2A
CAM 2B
CAM 4A

FIVE NIGHTS AT FREDDY'S:
SISTER
LOCATION

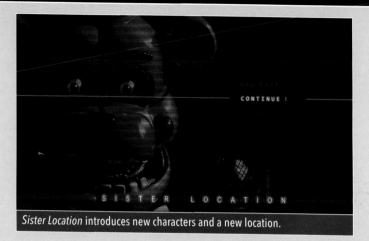

Sister Location introduces new characters and a new location.

Five Nights at Freddy's: Sister Location is the fifth installment of the *Five Nights at Freddy's* franchise. It was released on October 7, 2016. This is the first installment where the player can roam freely about the building. In *Five Nights at Freddy's: Sister Location*, you play as Michael Afton, the older son of William Afton, and the older brother of the crying boy. He is working the night shift at Circus Baby's Pizza World, a new pizzeria franchise that his father opened up to compete with Freddy Fazbear's Pizza. Michael's goal is to rescue his sister, who was killed by the animatronic his father built, Circus Baby.

In this game, players will not be staying in a single room to try and block animatronics from attacking them. They will have to complete predetermined tasks for each room as they maneuver their way through the pizzeria. The Funtime animatronics, following a circus theme, are introduced in this game. They are similar in color, featuring whites, pinks, and purples. Along with Funtime Freddy, Chica, Bonnie, and Foxy, there are some new characters as well. It is said that William Afton created these animatronics to kidnap and kill children more efficiently.

» CIRCUS BABY

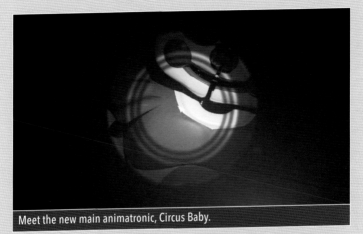

Meet the new main animatronic, Circus Baby.

She is the mascot and main antagonist of Circus Baby's Pizza World. Circus Baby's main objective is to count children. When there is only a single one left, she offers ice cream, and when they take it, she grabs them and kills them. Circus Baby is the animatronic that kills William Afton's daughter, Elizabeth Afton.

FAZBEAR FACT: YOU'LL HEAR CIRCUS BABY'S VOICE FOR THE FIRST TIME ON NIGHT 2. YOU'LL NOTICE THAT HER FRIENDLY, HELPFUL TONE TURNS MORE HOSTILE AS THE GAME PROGRESSES.

» BALLORA

Minireenas accompany Ballora in her gallery.

Ballora is a blue and white animatronic that looks like a ballerina. She was originally the star of the Ballora Gallery in Circus Baby's Entertainment and Rental.

» MINIREENAS

Minireenas travel alongside Ballora in her gallery. They're small, feminine-like mannequins, with thin frames and white faces. They do not have facial features that are incredibly detailed nor do they move around. They wear tutus and have their feet painted white to resemble shoes.

Bidybabs can attack the player with a devastating jumpscare.

The Bidybabs are a pair of animatronics that reside on stage with Circus Baby at the Circus Gallery. They're small, resembling babies. One of them has purple eyes while the other has green. They have a triangle nose, square teeth, and a button in the middle of their chest.

FAZBEAR FACT: SOME OF THE BIDYBABS' MEMORABLY CREEPY SAYINGS INCLUDE, "HELLO IN THERE" AND "I'M GOING TO FIND A WAY INSIDE."

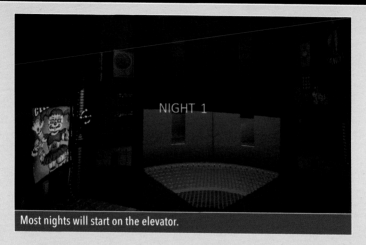

Most nights will start on the elevator.

On Night 1, you will meet HandUnit, which will give you your tasks for the night. Once you get off of the elevator and crawl through a vent, you'll be tasked with finding Ballora. When you check her stage, you'll notice that she isn't there. You'll have to shock her using the red button on the controlled shock keypad to get her attention. From there, you'll need to check on Funtime Foxy. You'll need to shock him twice to get him to appear on his stage.

Afterward, you'll have to travel to the Circus Control Area and look for Circus Baby. Upon checking for her multiple times, HandUnit will tell you she has made her way to the stage and you can end your shift and go home.

FAZBEAR FACT: IT IS IMPOSSIBLE FOR THE PLAYER TO BE JUMPSCARED ON NIGHT 1.

On Night 2, you will again start in an elevator and then crawl through a vent. This time, HandUnit will tell you that a dead body was found in that vent. The first task is to find Ballora again. As she is standing in front of the window and not on stage, HandUnit will encourage you to zap her.

Using the terminal, players can shock Ballora.

You then need to check on Funtime Foxy, who is also standing by the window. You'll have to find Circus Baby again like the night before and administer several unsuccessful shocks to her. Eventually, HandUnit will leave to turn the power back on.

Circus Baby will begin to speak to you. She will explain how she doesn't recognize you and ask why you decided to come. She will also tell you about a hiding spot that one of the other staff members made by carving a hole into their desk. You then have to go and try to hide in this spot.

Bidybab will try to confront you, so you'll need to remain hidden in this compartment. When you try to close the sliding door, if unsuccessful, you'll be jumpscared by Bidybab and then it's game over. After this happens, HandUnit will be back and instruct you to go to the Ballora Gallery to reach the Breaker Room and restore power to the place. Circus Baby will warn you that if you hear Ballora's music getting louder, you have to slow down so you don't get caught and attacked.

In Ballora's Gallery, you'll crawl through without drawing the animatronic's attention to survive the ordeal. Go toward the area with a dim light. Funtime Freddy will be waiting for you in the Breaker Room. While you fix the power, any animatronics nearby can attack you. The danger meter on the top of the screen will alert you to how close Funtime Freddy is to attacking you.

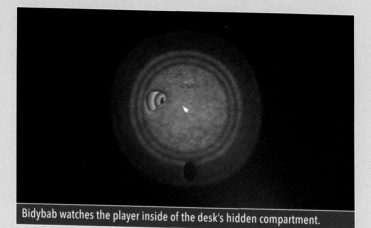

Bidybab watches the player inside of the desk's hidden compartment.

Funtime Freddy has a new vibrant look.

Just like with any *Five Nights at Freddy's* game, as the nights go on, the difficulty increases. Night 3 in *Sister Location* is no different. You will once again start in the elevator. Your task for the day is to check on Ballora first and then Funtime Foxy, who is not on his stage. You will be told by HandUnit not to check on Circus Baby, but if you decide to disobey him and check on her anyway you'll get unique dialogue where she tells you a little bit about the day she killed William Afton's daughter.

Afterward, you'll find yourself having to navigate a darkened Funtime Auditorium with a small light to get through to Parts and Services. Funtime Foxy is roaming about and if you bump into him, you'll reach a game over. The key to getting through this room is to maneuver slowly and keep your distance from Funtime Foxy. If he comes close to you, stop moving so he doesn't catch on to your location.

Once in Parts and Services, you'll have to help deactivate both Funtime Freddy and his puppet, Bon-Bon (the Funtime counterpart of Bonnie) by doing a few mini games. You'll then need to make your way through the Funtime Auditorium where a mandatory Funtime Foxy jumpscare will be triggered.

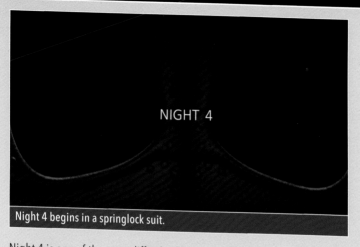

NIGHT 4

Night 4 begins in a springlock suit.

Night 4 is one of the most difficult of the game. Circus Baby will place you in a springlock suit, similar to the one that William Afton entered in *Five Nights at Freddy's 3*. In previous installments of the game, we found out that these animatronic suits are highly dangerous and very easily turned lethal if not used correctly. It is your job on Night 4 to survive being in this contraption without being skewered alive. Oh, did we mention the onslaught of little Minireenas who come your way?

This night takes place in the Scooper Room, where the animatronics are broken down and their endoskeletons removed. When Ballora is placed into the Scooper Room, she suffers an inevitable fate. It is up to you now to remain wound up in your springlock suit. To do so, you must click and hold the springlocks. All the while, Ballora's little Minireenas will crawl up your suit. You must shake them off so they don't kill you, but not enough that the springs on your suit will lock up and kill you.

This onslaught lasts for about three minutes. If you manage to get one of your springlocks unwound, you will be attacked and jumpscared by a Minireena. To beat this round, keep in mind there are only four waves of Minireenas to account for. When Circus Baby tells you to keep your springlocks wound up, immediately start doing so. There are five locks on each side. A good strategy is to go top to bottom starting with the left side and then going to the right. You may not have time to wind each lock up fully, but do enough that they will not completely run out.

Despite the cute and inviting look of Funtime Foxy, he is still rather scary!

Night 5 is the final night of the main story in *Five Nights at Freddy's: Sister Location*. There are two achievable endings. To unlock the bonus custom night, you'll need to achieve both of these endings and play through Circus Baby's secret mini game.

You'll need to fix Circus Baby's suit, as per her instructions. Once she gives you the code to open her suit, do so and enter the digits on the keypad. If you end up failing this mini game, a jumpscare will happen. However, there are two other options that will lead to different endings.

» TRUE ENDING

To get the True Ending you'll need to follow Circus Baby's exact instructions. Type the code in the keypad from Circus Baby's head. She will tell you that you need to go to the Scooper Room but to be careful that Ballora doesn't catch you. Once you reach the Scooper Room, you will see Ennard, an animatronic made of the merged endoskeleton of the other animatronics in the building. Ennard will apologize for misleading you and then use the Scooper to disembowel you and take the skin from Michael Afton's body. This is because, as Circus Baby said earlier, people will not accept the animatronics for who they are, so they must pretend to be someone else.

Circus Baby's mini game will tell players more of the *FNaF* lore.

Before you can reach the second ending of Five Nights at Freddy's: Sister Location, you must complete Circus Baby's mini game. Doing so will also unlock a star on the main menu as well as the Private Room survival game. To unlock the mini game you'll need to die about five times.

GAMEPLAY TIP: The easiest way to farm deaths is on Night 4 when trying to keep the springlocks wound up.

Once you trigger this mini game, you'll have to be very particular about how you complete it. You play as Circus Baby, who is giving out cupcakes to kids. You have a set amount of time to give out cupcakes to each kid. Failing to do so will end the mini game without unlocking anything.

There are three types of cupcakes. With the exception of the green one, each one needs to be shot at the kids twice for them to be satisfied and happy. The pink cupcake is an average cupcake that will go directly where you aim it. The blue one can reach three kids in a scattershot. The green cupcake reaches a long distance and will not disappear when you shoot it.

Meet William Afton's daughter in Circus Baby's mini game.

To complete this mini game, grab the pink cupcakes and head right. Feed the four kids that you see. Then, keep going right and jump on the top right platform. Feed pink cupcakes only to the kids on the platform. Ignore the ones on the ground, as you'll come back to them later. Jump over the top right platform and go past the blue cupcakes. Do not grab them. Instead, keep going and feed the first child two pink cupcakes. Go back to your left until you can grab the blue cupcakes. With those, go right and shoot them toward three kids on platforms. You will only need one shot if you position yourself properly and jump before firing. Keep going right and jump over the green cupcakes.

Feed the next three kids and then go back for the green cupcakes. Go left until you see the two kids on the ground who were not fed. Shoot the green cupcakes at them. Now, keep going right until you see two kids by two ledges. Jump carefully so as not to fall as you move right. Feed the kids and keep moving right until you see an ice cream cone. This will only appear if you have fed all available kids.

With the ice cream in hand, your time will have slowed down considerably. Go all the way to the left until you reach the very first screen. Place the ice cream down between two flowers and approach the left side of the screen. Elizabeth Afton will approach Circus Baby, who will extend a claw from her chest and kill the young girl.

» FAKE ENDING

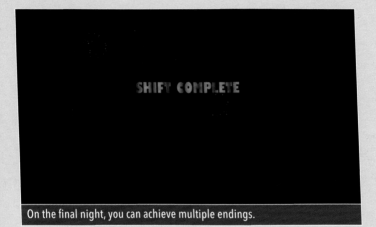

On the final night, you can achieve multiple endings.

You can achieve the Fake Ending by ignoring Circus Baby's instructions. This will only be triggered if you have beaten the second stage of the Circus Baby mini game, because you need to have unlocked the Private Room. Ignoring Circus Baby's instructions leads to a much more pleasant outcome for Michael Afton, but it's not the canon ending, meaning the official ending according to the creator.

Once you step away from Circus Baby's keypad, you can make your way to the Private Room. You'll be locked in to complete a night similar to the original *Five Nights at Freddy's* game, where you'll need to fend off Ennard until 6 a.m. You will have three things to keep an eye on: the security monitor, the doors, and the front vent.

Ennard will use a lot of different tactics, including talking to Michael Afton as his little sister Elizabeth, who has long since taken over Circus Baby's body when she was murdered by the animatronic. At the end of this level, you will be transported home, where you will watch the last episode of your television show and Ennard slinks across the screen.

The player is joined by Ennard in their home at the end of the game.

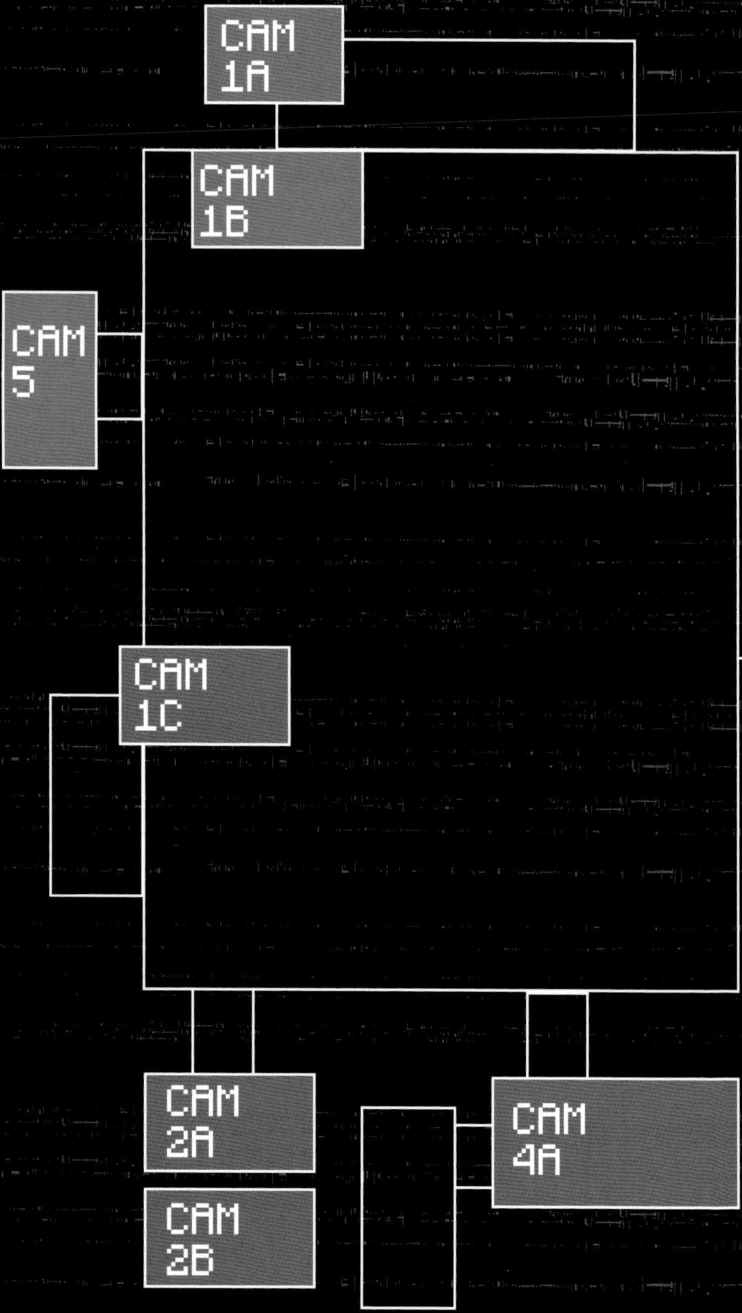
CAM 1A
CAM 1B
CAM 5
CAM 1C
CAM 2A
CAM 2B
CAM 4A

FREDDY FAZBEAR'S
PIZZERIA
SIMULATOR

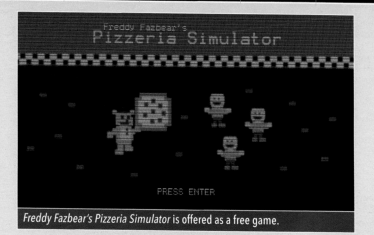

Freddy Fazbear's Pizzeria Simulator is offered as a free game.

Freddy Fazbear's Pizzeria Simulator is the sixth game in the *Five Nights at Freddy's* franchise. It takes place directly after the events of *Five Nights at Freddy's 3*. The main goal of this game is to run a successful pizzeria business with no incidents. At night, however, you'll need to fend off the murderous animatronics while you complete your tasks. You once again play as Michael Afton, who was reanimated after Ennard ejected itself from his body in the last game.

In this game, the player will have to pick and choose items to add to their pizzeria. You want to choose items that will yield money and no liability. As the game progresses, you'll have the option to salvage animatronics found in the alleyway. If you do, you can gain more money for your business. However, this makes it difficult at night, when you have to fend off more animatronics. You'll meet Cassette Man, also known as Henry, who will aid you in the salvaging process.

Become the owner of your very own Freddy Fazbear franchise.

At night you'll need to pay attention to a few things to ward off the animatronics. There is a computer that you need to complete your tasks and a fan that you can use to cool down the Office. If it reaches 120 degrees Fahrenheit, you will pass out and end the night poorly. However, using the fan and the computer creates noise, which attracts the animatronics to the Office. Advertisement deals can also appear as pop-ups on the screen that you will have to close out. You will also have access to flashlights to shine at the vents to scare animatronics away. There are also audio lures you can use as distractions.

FAZBEAR FACT: *FREDDY FAZBEAR'S PIZZERIA SIMULATOR* IS THE FIRST GAME IN THE FRANCHISE TO INCLUDE MORE THAN FIVE NIGHTS IN THE MAIN STORY. IT ALSO DOES NOT INCLUDE THE "FIVE NIGHTS" TRADEMARK IN THE TITLE.

Purchasing certain discounted items will invite aggressive animatronics into your establishment.

Day 1 gives you $100 to start. You can buy anything you'd like from the catalog. However, if you buy the sale version of the Discount Ball Pit you can summon Molten Freddy into your establishment early. This will add an extra challenge. You can also opt into a sponsorship with Fiztime Pop Soda. This will earn you an extra $250 but will provide pop-ups to fight off during the night.

This night acts as a tutorial day to help you familiarize yourself with the game's mechanics. The tutorial unit will show you where the animatronics will attack you from in the vents. If you did not purchase the Discount Ball Pit, you will have no animatronics to worry about and the day will go smoothly. You'll need to do your management tasks and log off. If you did purchase the Discount Ball Pit, however, you'll need to be careful to protect yourself from the roaming animatronics.

Salvage different animatronics or leave them in the alley you found them in.

Molten Freddy is a version of Ennard with Funtime Freddy taking charge instead of Circus Baby. As such, his tactics are very much like Funtime Freddy's. As it is the first day, focusing on exploring the game's mechanics will be most beneficial. You will not be able to close the doors to the Office, so actively use your audio lures and flashlight to help keep animatronics at bay.

During the daytime you'll want to use most, if not all, of your play tokens. This way you can earn new items and new catalogs, as they'll unlock with the more things you buy. You need to buy items to not only entertain your guests but also help with sanitation and health. This will help you earn more money in the long term.

Scrap Baby is a new animatronic introduced in *Freddy Fazbear's Pizzeria Simulator*.

Molten Freddy is hiding in the Discount Ball Pit.

You have the option to salvage Molten Freddy in the alley. If you choose not to, he will not appear in the night unless you purchase the Discount Ball Pit where he is hiding. You can buy Nedd Bear from the catalog, which will introduce Scraptrap to your pizzeria. You can also opt in to another sponsorship. Scraptrap is another iteration of William Afton, this time in the form of a badly damaged and decrepit yellow bunny. You can see most of William's flesh and bones in this animatronic suit as opposed to Springtrap, where you see mostly machinery.

You will be able to use a motion tracker, audio lures, and a silent vent system to help get through the night. The motion tracker will identify the animatronics' movements, the audio lure can get the animatronics to move to another room, and the silent vent system will make less noise. Make sure that during the day you purchase as many things to help make your tasks as easy as possible. Use the audio lure to move the animatronics away from your location, and turn off your PC and vent system if this does not work. Once your temperature rises, turn the fan back on.

Scraptrap is another animatronic you can salvage. But every night after that, he will try to attack the office whether you are successful or not.

On Day 3, if you purchase the marked-down version of the Star Curtain Stage, you will gain another animatronic, Scrap Baby. Scrap Baby is a damaged and recycled version of Circus Baby. She has a bluish tint to her skin and bright orange hair. She wears roller skates and a tiara.

Focus on purchasing items that will help make completing your tasks easier. This will make focusing on keeping the animatronics out of the Office a bigger priority. Be sure to flash any animatronics that crawl through the vent toward you. If they are close, turn off your computer and fan to make less noise. Use an audio lure to get the animatronic to leave the vents and travel somewhere else. At the end of this day, if you don't already have Scrap Baby, you'll have the option to salvage her or throw her away in the alley.

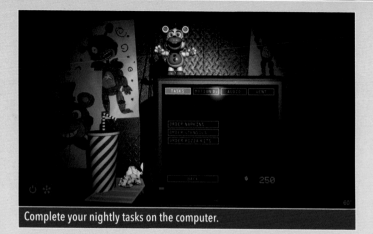

Complete your nightly tasks on the computer.

On Day 4, you can purchase Lefty from the "Rare Finds Auction" catalog. This will allow him to enter the pizzeria early. With up to four animatronics roaming around, you will have a difficult time trying to complete your tasks and also ward off the animatronics. If you turn off your PC, the animatronics will pay less attention to you. However, it will cut into your time completing tasks. Use your audio lure to get the animatronics away from the vent and the Office and use the motion sensor to track their movements.

You can take different sponsorship opportunities to make money, however it makes the game harder.

On Days 5 and 6, repeat the same strategies you used on Day 4. Keep in mind that from Day 4 on, you will potentially have all animatronics available, so you'll want to make sure the Office is making as little noise as possible. Buy items in the catalog that will help reduce the amount of noise you are making. Also be wary of taking on sponsorships. You will get more money for them, but they will pop up on the screen until you close them.

GAMEPLAY TIP: If you have the available funds, purchase as many upgrades as you can to make your tasks easier.

You can obtain one of seven endings.

» COMPLETION ENDING

To get this ending, you must salvage all of the animatronics from the alley and avoid going bankrupt. Once achieved, you will hear Scrap Baby say she will make her father, William Afton, proud by attempting to kill more children. However, Henry, the father of one of the children who was murdered in William's first attack, tells her that the pizzeria was a labyrinth all along and they would not be able to reach any children. Instead, he gathers all the animatronics together into the building and apologizes to his daughter for not being able to save her. He wants to atone and does so by burning all the remains of the animatronics, freeing their souls.

He tells the player at the very end of the cutscene, "There is no need for you to return to work next week, as Fazbear Entertainment is no longer a corporate entity." You'll receive a certificate of completion that will display on the title screen.

» THE BAD ENDING

This ending is unlocked when the player has failed to salvage at least one animatronic in the back alley. The man on the cassette player will congratulate you for completing your shift but then fire you for not completing your "special obligations under Paragraph 4."

» THE MEDIOCRE ENDING

Earn the Certificate of Mediocrity in the "Mediocre Ending."

You get this ending by not investing any money in the pizzeria. Your final Faz-Rating has to be zero. The Tutorial Unit will call you lazy and grant you the Certificate of Mediocrity, which will unlock on the main menu.

» BLACKLISTED ENDING

This ending is unlocked when the player has a liability risk of fifty or higher on the last day. The Tutorial Unit will congratulate you for wanting to take risks, but you are considered a liability hazard and will receive a certificate saying you are blacklisted.

» BANKRUPTCY ENDING

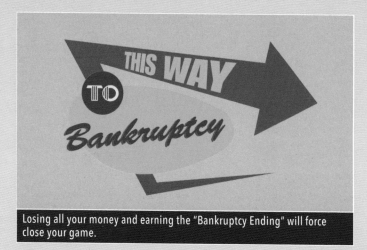

Losing all your money and earning the "Bankruptcy Ending" will force close your game.

This ending is achieved when the player loses all their money by investing in a lawsuit. You will receive a certificate of bankruptcy and the game will force close. You will then have to beat the Freddy Pizza mini game in the beginning again.

» INSANITY ENDING

This can be earned by having the Egg Baby item placed inside the pizzeria. Place the Egg Baby, then go to your terminal and hold down the cursor on the bottom left of the screen until secret blueprints show up. You will hear Cassette Man's plan from the Completion Ending and be reprimanded for poking around where you shouldn't. You will be fired and given the Certificate of Insanity so no one will believe what you've heard.

» LOREKEEPER ENDING

You can reach this ending by playing the Security Puppet mini game a total of three times, by going to the gap in lap 4 during the *Midnight Motorist* mini game, and by playing the *Fruity Maze* mini game without achieving a game over. You'll also need to salvage all of the animatronics. This will earn you a copy of the image from the Completion Ending.

Play several mini games to gain more knowledge of the *FNAF* world.

Each mini game can be completed in two ways. By doing special tasks, you're able to unlock secret bits of lore to help understand *Five Nights at Freddy's* story better.

» FRUIT MAZE ARCADE

To unlock the secret lore in this game, you need to collect all of the fruit successfully three times.

» MIDNIGHT MOTORIST

Look for a hole at the bottom of the track that will appear after a few laps. Enter this hole and take the left at the fork in the road.

» SECURITY PUPPET

When you're trapped, wait until you're set free and then head to the door. Help the child who is waiting directly in front of you.

» CANDY CADET

You'll want to keep play testing this game, even if it means using all your play tokens, so you can unlock new dialogue.

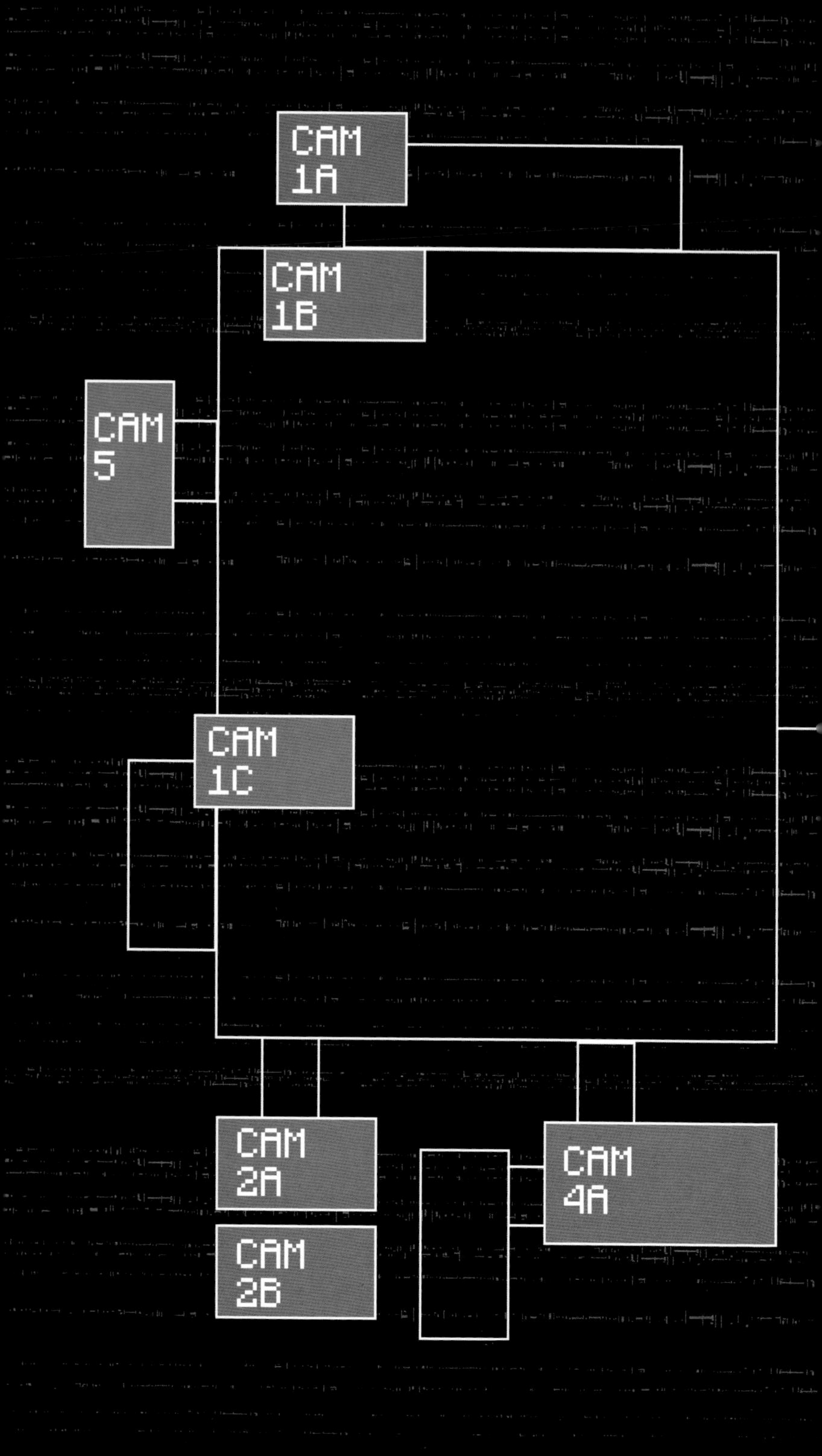
CAM 1A
CAM 1B
CAM 5
CAM 1C
CAM 2A
CAM 2B
CAM 4A

OTHER GAMES

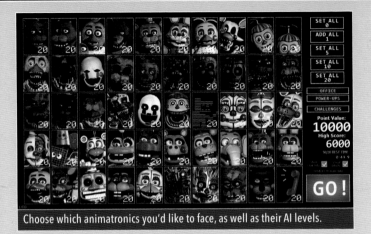

Choose which animatronics you'd like to face, as well as their AI levels.

This is the last game of the *Five Nights at Freddy's* franchise that allows players to customize the levels of the animatronic AIs. In this version of the game, you're allowed to pick from a host of fifty animatronics that you've met across the series. These include favorites like the Toy animatronics, Nightmare animatronics, and Funtime animatronics. Each animatronic has their own tactics and voiced lines in the game. You're able to choose just about any combination of animatronics and difficulty level.

The player will always be put into the Office with two vents, two side doors, a security monitor, a Freddy Fazbear head, and two hoses. There's also a noise meter, a heat meter, and other features like pop-up advertisements that you'll need to click away. You'll need to pay attention to what each animatronic does to be able to ward them off. There are various challenges on the "Challenge" menu that you can choose from as well as unlockable cutscenes and designs for the Office. This is a great way to practice going up against your toughest opponents.

FAZBEAR FACT: *ULTIMATE CUSTOM NIGHT* WAS ORIGINALLY MEANT TO RELEASE AS AN ADDITION FOR *FREDDY FAZBEAR'S PIZZERIA SIMULATOR*.

Help Wanted is the first *FNAF* game that can be played with a VR headset.

This is the first game in the series to be ported to virtual reality. However, you can play without a virtual reality headset if you'd like. In this game, Fazbear Entertainment has tried to create a virtual reality experience for their fans in an attempt to win back a positive reputation and clear their name. Unfortunately however, a malevolent glitch was released into the game files by the name of Glitchtrap, a version of Spring Bonnie.

You'll be able to play through forty mini games that are inspired from the previous games in the franchise. You'll be able to interact with Freddy, Bonnie, Chica, Foxy, Springtrap, Mangle, Funtime Foxy, and Circus Baby. *Five Nights at Freddy's 1* inspired five mini games that are related to the five original nights. *Five Nights at Freddy's 4* inspired mini games that include trying to prevent animatronics from entering a child's bedroom. Nine mini games are inspired by *Five Nights at Freddy's: Sister Location*. Players will need to repair animatronics, maintenance areas, and more.

As the story goes on, you'll find tapes that, when pieced together, release the malicious code that created Glitchtrap, a virtual version of William Afton that was taken from Springtrap's circuit board. Glitchtrap wants to escape this virtual reality game by joining with the player.

Glitchtrap is the game's main antagonist.

Complete all of the mini games to unlock different endings and earn hidden cassette tapes that will fill you in on game lore. You can also earn coins to unlock virtual prizes. When you complete each mini game you'll unlock a much harder game mode, called Blacklight mode, that adds more distractions for players. If you can beat each mini game in both regular and Blacklight mode, you'll unlock one last mini game called Pizza Party.

Five Nights at Freddy's: Help Wanted has four possible endings the player can achieve.

» NORMAL ENDING

The first ending is achievable by finishing all forty mini games, including Pizza Party. You will enter a dark room where Glitchtrap will beckon for you to approach him behind a curtain. When you do so, you'll find yourself stuffed in a Freddy animatronic suit while Glitchtrap dances in the back.

» MASK ENDING

The second ending is achieved by following the instructions found on each of the audio tapes. Players will be brought to a cryptic room. Glitchtrap will show himself briefly before telling you to be quiet and backing into the darkness. You will receive a plushie of Glitchtrap. If you have completed the secret ending of the mini game *Curse of Dreadbear*, you'll receive a rabbit mask as well. Combining the mask and the plushie will reveal who the player character is and how they are working for William Afton.

» MERGE ENDING

The third ending happens if the player does not follow the instructions on the audio tapes. This will end up with Glitchtrap swapping bodies with the player.

» PRINCESS QUEST ENDING

This ending is exclusive only to the mobile version of the game because you'll need to complete the special Princess Quest level. In this ending, you take the role of the Princess who confronts Glitchtrap.

CAM
1A

CAM
1B

CAM
5

CAM
1C

CAM
2A

CAM
2B

CAM
4A

FIVE NIGHTS AT FREDDY'S:
SECURITY
BREACH

Glamrock Freddy is a friendly animatronic that will help Gregory on his journey.

Unlike the other installments in the *Five Nights at Freddy's* franchise, *Security Breach* is a free roam game that takes place across a single night. You play as a young boy named Gregory, who was trapped inside of the Freddy Fazbear's Mega Pizzaplex. You team up with Glamrock Freddy Fazbear to escape the attack of many new and reimagined animatronics. This is the first game in the series where you can see a third-person view of your player character and the only game where you maneuver through a single night.

Gregory will have to use the building's security cameras, hiding spots, advice from Freddy, and more, to keep him alive for the night. In this game, you'll need to explore the Mega Pizzaplex and uncover its secrets in order to survive. Complete all the missions assigned to you and figure out how to fight off animatronics that get stronger as the night progresses.

There are over thirty missions to complete in the game. Use the tricks that follow to master the most difficult ones and get through the game in one piece!

Montgomery, Chica, and Roxy are all animatronics that Gregory will have to run away from in order to survive the night at the Pizzaplex. If you confront these bosses and defeat them, you will earn parts that you can use to upgrade Glamrock Freddy later on in the game. These upgrades will make completing missions easier.

» S.T.A.F.F. BOTS

The Party Bot will remain friendly if Gregory has a Party Pass.

Avoid S.T.A.F.F. bots as you venture throughout the Pizzaplex. The S.T.A.F.F. bots are automated robots that patrol the Mega Pizzaplex. Unlike the animatronics, these bots move around on wheels and do not have legs. If you're not careful, they'll deliver some terrifying jumpscares.

A S.T.A.F.F. bot's color will vary depending on its role. Some are waiters, cleaning staff, and even security guards. The most common kind are the security variants that patrol the Pizzaplex at night. They move around the area, projecting a beam of light. If Gregory wanders into this light, the player will earn a jumpscare and the nearby animatronics will hear the noise. Take note of the set path that the bots travel on and learn to avoid them.

Map bots can jumpscare Gregory without prompt, but they are harmless and will not alert the nearby animatronics to his location. They will remain peaceful so long as Gregory heeds their warning to "exit the premises." Otherwise, they'll ring an alarm that the animatronics will hear.

There are a variety of other bots that the player can run into, so be careful when interacting with them! Some are more dangerous than others.

» CHICA

You can defeat Glamrock Chica to earn the ability to unlock certain areas.

This fight will unlock after 4 a.m., where Gregory will have the choice to either fight Chica or Montgomery Gator. Defeating either one will grant you an upgrade part for Glamrock Freddy. Chica's upgrade will allow you to unlock certain doors. This is one of the less useful powers, but it is a solid upgrade to have if you're a "completionist" and want to unlock everything the game has to offer.

To be able to take out Chica once and for all, you'll need to be in possession of the Monty Mystery Mix. You'll have found this item behind the ice cream counter in the back of the Bonnie Bowl attraction. However, to gain access to Bonnie Bowl you'll need to get the Bonnie Bowl Pass from Fazer Blast during the 4 a.m. hour.

Once you have the Monty Mystery Mix, you can go to the bottom level of the Atrium and head through a door on your right side (when you're looking away from the vent that you would use to access the Loading Dock). Keep heading that way and you'll eventually reach the Loading Dock's kitchen where you can find Chica guarding a power generator in a nearby storage room. As Gregory, exit Glamrock Freddy and sneak up to the generator. Turn it on, and dash out of the area towards the exit on the west side of the room. Chica will have begun chasing you, so utilize your surroundings, including the storage rooms, to get back to the front of the kitchen. You'll want to place the Monty Mystery Mix in the trash compactor in the area and then press the button to activate it.

This will activate a cutscene showing Chica getting crushed by the trash compactor. This does not mean the fight is over, however. This will actually officially activate Chica's boss fight. Once the cutscene is over, you'll awaken in the sewer.

GAMEPLAY TIP: If you approach Chica's remains, you can take her beak and then move forward to a save station. Be sure to use the beak before the real boss battle begins!

The fight will start once you switch on the generator. You'll want to jump right into a nearby parts and service bin to hide before Chica makes her way into the room. Chica will be able to move her head all the way around, so she can spot you in any direction. On the other hand, she makes much louder noises, so you'll be able to locate her without the use of cameras. You'll want to wait until Chica is away from you, which you'll know by using your cameras or listening to her location, and then run to the exit. Chica will not chase you during this section, so move at your own pace. However, she will be waiting at the very end of the path. You'll have two ways to get past her. You can either shoot her with the Fazer Blaster to stun her, or run around her using the metal walkway. Keep moving, avoiding the trash beneath you, until you get to a locked gate and a save station. The tunnel on your left will lead to your next destination.

You'll be trying to avoid running into Chica as you navigate through tunnels. Look for the generator in the back left corner of the area. Once there, turn it off and head back to the entrance. Your last generator to turn off will be in the parking lot. Utilize the various hiding spots to avoid Chica.

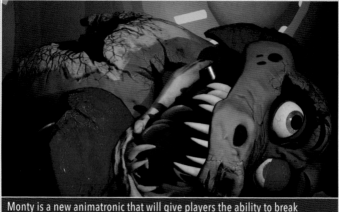

Monty is a new animatronic that will give players the ability to break through area blocks.

By defeating Montgomery Gator, you'll gain an upgrade which will allow you to break through chain fences and closed gates. You'll be able to get his claws by completing a boss battle that will be accessible by completing the Mazercize puzzle in Monty's Gator Golf.

Monty is one of the hardest bosses to fight, but it isn't impossible to beat him. Outside of Mazercise, you'll be able to use the turret to activate the boss battle. However, be sure to save your game first!

Montgomery Gator has a jumping attack that can be pretty lethal, so avoiding it altogether is your best bet of survival. Unfortunately, because of Monty's shades, you can't stun him using the Fazer Blaster. To defeat Monty, you want to access all of the turrets in the surrounding area in order to fill up the splash bucket on the left side of the arena. When the splash bucket is full, run towards the button near it and a cutscene will play. Then, you'll be able to grab his claws.

> **GAMEPLAY TIP:** Do not stay crouched, as hiding will not work on Monty. Continuing to run around will be the most effective. Use the corners of the arena is also helpful, as they can help Monty lose sight of you as he chases you through the walkway.

GAMEPLAY TIP: When you reach a turret, make sure to use up all ten balls as they will not regenerate until there are none left.

» ROXY

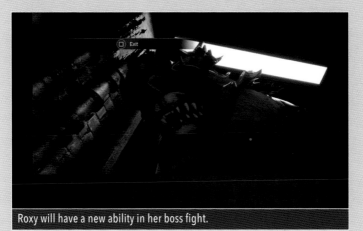

Roxy will have a new ability in her boss fight.

By defeating Roxy, you'll gain an upgrade which will allow you to see through walls. To trigger this boss battle, you will have to head to Roxy's Raceway after 5 a.m. Make sure that you have fixed the go-kart, or else you won't be able to fight Roxy. Be sure to save your game first and then approach the green button near the save station. When you first spot Roxy, move to the left so that she'll run through the wooden door in front of you.

Because of earlier events in the story, this version of Roxy will not have eyes. This will make it much easier for you to sneak around her because she won't be able to see very far. However, this version of Roxy will also be much more unpredictable and aggressive in her actions.

GAMEPLAY TIP: You'll want to keep an eye on Roxy's charge attack. She'll drop to the ground and a sound will emit from her. So, when you see or hear her get into position, prepare yourself. You'll be able to dodge the attack, or you'll be able to outrun it.

You'll want to run more often than not so that you can bait Roxy into knocking into wooden blockades that are in your way. You'll also be able to use noise in the form of distractions to get her attention. When you enter the last area, the Furnace, things will be slightly different. You won't be able to run through the flames even though Roxy's pace doesn't slow down. A good strategy will be to bait a charge attack from Roxy when you're at the front of the room. When she gets close, you can run around Roxy and towards the vent on the other side of the room where you'll be able to escape.

GAMEPLAY TIP: 5 a.m. is the last hour where you'll be able to save the game. Utilize this hour to get any collectibles or upgrade parts that you're looking for.

In this game, the player will reunite with Vanny, who is revealed to be the beta tester from *Five Nights at Freddy's: Help Wanted*. You'll get the chance to explore a total of six endings, which will reveal different information and earn you a different number of stars.

PRO TIPS

* Save your game often!

* Familiarize yourself with the mall's hiding spots.

* Check the security cameras often.

* Use audio cues to help locate the animatronics.

* Use Glamrock Freddy to your advantage.

* Get the Fazer Blaster and Faz Camera.

In the Redemption Ending, Gregory will be able to escape the Pizzaplex with Glamrock Freddy.

» THE ALLEY ENDING

This is triggered if Gregory chooses to leave through the front entrance at 6 a.m. Gregory will return to the alley where he lives. He'll put a newspaper over his body with pictures of the missing children from the Pizzaplex, all while Vanny is looming overhead.

» THE GETAWAY ENDING

This is triggered if Gregory leaves through the loading dock. He will recharge Glamrock Freddy's battery with the power from a van he steals. It is later revealed that the animatronic is replaced in the Pizzaplex with another.

» BURNTRAP ENDING

This ending will only be possible if Gregory defeats Monty or Chica and fully upgrades Freddy. Then, he and Freddy can go to the bottom of Roxy's Raceway and find the remains of the pizza place from Freddy Fazbear's Pizzeria Simulator. William Afton will reveal himself in the form of Burntrap, and it will become clear how he brainwashed Vanny. He and Gregory will fight, but parts of the building collapsing will cause Gregory and Freddy to flee. Burntrap will be dragged away, and his location will remain unknown.

» THE FINAL BOSS ENDING

William Afton returns to the latest installment of *Five Nights at Freddy's*.

During this fight, you'll also be up against the other animatronics. Afton will not physically harm Gregory; however, he will try to control Freddy by placing his hand on monitors around the three rooms he will maneuver through. To stop this, you'll need to find the monitor that Afton is on, and press the button next to it to burn him.

In phase one, you'll want to listen to Freddy's warnings of which animatronic has entered the chamber. Focus on burning Afton using the monitors until you hear which animatronic is in the room. If Afton was burned using the left or right monitors, he'll be waiting at the middle monitor. If he walks upwards, it means he'll be going to the left monitor, and if he goes downwards on the middle monitor, he'll be moving to the right monitor next.

If Freddy calls out Chica's name, look for her. When she approaches close enough, close the door on her. She'll bang on the door for a few moments until she saunters off and you can unlock the door and go back to the monitors. If Freddy tells you to look out for the vents, go to the vent that is next to the middle monitor and lock it. Monty will usually appear here and bang for a few moments before giving up and leaving. Then, you can unlock the vents and go back to the monitors.

If you hear Roxy crying, listen closely. When she's close to you, you can use Chica's voice box to scare her away. However, keep an eye on the monitors prior and make sure Afton hasn't tried to attack Freddy. During these encounters, Freddy can lose power or even eject Gregory from his suit so keep an eye on those parameters.

In Phase Two, tentacles will rise from the ground and drop from the ceiling. In this phase you'll want to avoid touching the tentacles while also trying to repel Afton on the monitors. He can revert back to phase one at any given moment, so be aware of what is happening in this fight. Being in Freddy's suit makes you immune to the tentacles, which can help you maneuver to certain hard-to-reach monitors.

Keep this up until you burn Afton enough times for a cutscene to play. This is the true canon ending.

» TO THE ROOFTOP ENDING

This is triggered if you can gather enough collectibles and have upgraded Freddy. Gregory and Freddy want to burn down the Pizzaplex, but are stopped by Vanny when they are on the roof. Freddy tackles Vanny off of the roof, destroying them both and revealing Vanny to be a woman who looks eerily familiar to Vanessa, the security guard of the Pizzaplex. This path ends in the Pizzaplex burning down entirely.

» DISASSEMBLE VANNY ENDING

You can approach Vanny in Fazer Blast to fight. Her robots will disassemble Freddy, forcing Gregory to face her on his own. Gregory will be able to grab this device and have Vanny disassembled. Pizzaplex closes for the season.

» REDEMPTION ENDING

Gregory can complete three Princess Quest arcade games. This will lead him down the path of not killing Vanny. Instead, he will find out that the robots in the mall have been shut down completely and Vanny's mask is missing. Gregory and the security guard, Vanessa, escape and eat ice cream together.

» INDEX